VINTAGE
Christmas

———• ✳ •———

VINTAGE
Christmas

HOLIDAY STORIES FROM RURAL PEI

—◦— ✳ —◦—

MARLENE CAMPBELL

NIMBUS
PUBLISHING

Nimbus Publishing Limited
3731 Mackintosh St, Halifax, NS B3K 5A5
(902) 455-4286 nimbus.ca

Printed and bound in Canada

NB1223

FSC
www.fsc.org

MIX
Paper from
responsible sources
FSC® C013916

Cover illustration: Bigstock.com
Cover and interior design: Jenn Embree

Library and Archives Canada Cataloguing in Publication

Campbell, Marlene, author
Vintage Christmas : holiday stories from rural PEI / collected and retold by Marlene Campbell.
Issued in print and electronic formats.
ISBN 978-1-77108-450-5 (paperback).--ISBN 978-1-77108-451-2 (html)
    1. Christmas--Prince Edward Island. I. Title.

GT4987.15.C23 2016   394.266309717   C2016-903744-4
                                             C2016-903745-2

Canada

Canada Council Conseil des arts
for the Arts   du Canada

Nimbus Publishing acknowledges the financial support for its publishing activities from the Government of Canada through the Canada Book Fund (CBF) and the Canada Council for the Arts, and from the Province of Nova Scotia. We are pleased to work in partnership with the Province of Nova Scotia to develop and promote our creative industries for the benefit of all Nova Scotians.

To my mother, Glen, and my late father, Gordon, who made
Christmas special for their five children.

Table of Contents

INTRODUCTION · 1

VERA'S CHRISTMAS AWAY FROM HOME (1929) · · · · · · · · · 4

THE UNFORGETTABLE CHRISTMAS (1931) · · · · · · · · · · · 12

THE CHRISTMAS SPIRIT OF 1934 · · · · · · · · · · · · · · · 23

PLUM PUDDING CHRISTMAS (1935) · · · · · · · · · · · · · · 29

GORDON'S CHRISTMAS SKATES (1936) · · · · · · · · · · · · 41

A CHRISTMAS GOODBYE (1941) · · · · · · · · · · · · · · · · 51

LAURA'S WORST CHRISTMAS (1941) · · · · · · · · · · · · · 59

A TEST OF CHRISTMAS FAITH (1942) · · · · · · · · · · · · · 67

OLGA RETURNS HOME FOR CHRISTMAS (1942) · · · · · · · · 74

GRANDMA MAGGIE (1943) · · · · · · · · · · · · · · · · · · 84

A SURPRISE VISIT TO TOWN (1945) · · · · · · · · · · · · · 91

A WINTER ADVENTURE ON SKIS (1946) · · · · · · · · · · · 100

THE CHRISTMAS CONCERT (1946) · · · · · · · · · · · · · · 109

THE BELLS (1948) · 116

CHRISTMAS FROM THE ASHES (1949) · · · · · · · · · · · · 122

THE SPIRIT OF AN EVERGREEN (1950) · · · · · · · · · · · · 128

THE GIRLS SELECT THE TREE (1963) · · · · · · · · · · · · · 138

A BIKE TO GROW INTO (1964) · · · · · · · · · · · · · · · · 142

ACKNOWLEDGEMENTS · 151

Introduction

I did not intentionally set out to write a book. I wrote my first Christmas story in December 2004 when I wanted to create a public program that would offer a tranquil and reflective approach to the busy holiday season. I wanted an authentic Prince Edward Island tale that a local audience would embrace. This is no easy task in a province where the art of storytelling is enthusiastically practiced and celebrated. As a child, I thought there was nothing better than to be in the presence of adults as they conversed; I learned to sit quietly and absorb their stories.

I had little time to prepare for my program and needed inspiration. I wondered if I had a personal Christmas memory that stood out in my mind. It didn't take long to write the 1964 story, "A Bike to Grow Into." The audience responded positively when I read it aloud in the quiet, softly lit, historic church sanctuary. Memories were triggered. June Hutchinson MacLean, a friend and neighbour, approached me after the service and revealed her own Christmas story—several in fact. (You'll find three of them in this collection.) The following Christmas, I turned to her for inspiration. One question led to another and I realized I was unearthing far more than stories;

I was discovering the long-lost traditions, values, and lifestyles of Prince Edward Islanders.

I realized everyone has a story and I needed to start asking questions of my own elders while there was still time. The things I learned gave me great appreciation for their resourcefulness and determination, as well as a greater understanding of family dynamics. It soon became natural for me to ask seniors, "Do you have a Christmas story tucked away?" I usually received the same answer: "No, I have nothing worth telling."

Thankfully, I am a persistent person. Bit by bit, question by question, I brought stories to light. The process helped me accept my curiosity (some might call it "nosiness") as a good thing; it helped me give a voice to those who thought their memories were uninteresting.

Year after year, I added one or two stories to my collection for the annual community Christmas program. They were read aloud, enjoyed, and then filed away. As the number of stories grew, my friend and co-worker Jean MacKay—who had helped me prepare the stories for oral presentation—encouraged me to submit them to a publisher for consideration. Another co-worker, Carol MacFarlane, encouraged me to find an avenue to share them with a wider audience. It took me until the fall of 2014 to find both the courage and time to submit a sample to Nimbus Publishing. I am grateful for their positive response and have had the privilege of working with editor Emily MacKinnon to present this collection based on the experiences of real Prince Edward Islanders.

I am deeply indebted to the individuals who trusted me to enter their personal lives to capture, and set into context, a treasured Christmas memory. Without them, there would be no book. I hope future generations will be appreciative of their willingness to share. I also hope that their recollections, both happy and nostalgic, will bring joy to readers young and old and those in between.

I am still asking people for stories.

Vera's Christmas Away from Home

(1929)

THIS STORY WAS WRITTEN AFTER A PLEASURABLE INTER-
VIEW WITH VERA YEO FORBES IN THE FALL OF 2012. THAT
CHRISTMAS, VERA GREATLY ENJOYED HEARING THE STORY READ
ALOUD AT A SPECIAL EVENING OF STORIES AND CAROLS HELD AT
HER CHURCH, LOT 16 UNITED. VERA DIED IN JANUARY 2015.

I laid down my knife and fork and eased back in my chair to survey the dining room. As a recent newcomer to the nursing home, I watched for a signal that it would be appropriate to rise and go back to my small room. Within seconds, care workers began to move those seated in wheelchairs. Then the rest of us rose from our seats. I steadied myself with the aid of my newly acquired walker and joined the procession heading down the hallway into the main lobby, which branched off into the nursing wings. It occurred to me that we must look as though we were in a walker marathon.

Just as I reached the lobby, I saw a person waiting for me and knew immediately why she had come. Marlene, a local writer, was always searching for a new story and was sure I could provide her with inspiration. I did not share her confidence and had been able to avoid her request for an interview on previous occasions. My first excuse was a trip to Yellowknife where my daughter lives. When I came back from my visit I excused myself again, suggesting I needed time to rest. Then came a fall, which landed me in the hospital for an extensive stay, followed by family and medical consultations about what was best for me. Soon I found myself in the situation of leaving my residence and accepting the care offered in the nursing home.

So now I was caught, with no excuse to offer. She was standing right there and I will admit I welcomed the distraction. I didn't even bother with a greeting.

"Okay, let's get this over with. Come on down to my room." She nodded and fell in behind me. Once we were comfortably seated, I said, "So what is it you want to know?" And so it began—she wanted me to tell her about my most memorable Christmas.

Well, I thought, *that won't be difficult*. I knew exactly which Christmas was the most memorable. Despite the fact that I was only a few days short of my ninety-third birthday, my memory was still as sharp as a tack. As I settled into the story that was welling up in my mind, the mundane smells and sounds of my current surroundings gave way to the powerful memory of the Christmas of 1929.

That particular Christmas I was ten years old and growing up on a farm in southwest Prince Edward Island: Lot 16, overlooking the Grand River. My family was cash poor, but I wasn't aware of that because I had parents who cared for me, good food on the table, a comfortable bed, and a nickel in my pocket each Sunday to put in the collection plate. Up to the age of eight, I was an only child. Then, mysteriously, a brother arrived to be part of the family. Though the age difference between us was significant, he caused little disruption in my world.

My life revolved around friends, school, church, and the farm. I basically lived in the barn. There were always kittens to be played with, and calves, piglets, and lambs to be fed. If Father was not about, I would disobey his orders and climb up on a barrel to curry the workhorse. I would run the brush over his heavy shoulders and curving back, loving the feel of his strength beneath my small hands as I breathed in the wonderful smell of his hair and skin.

When I wasn't in the barn or doing chores for my mother in the house, I entertained myself with outdoor play. The changing seasons brought opportunities for swimming down at the shore in summer and sledding on the hill behind the house or skating on the field ponds in winter.

Christmas was a special time and a busy time. The teacher in the one-room schoolhouse would distribute parts for the Christmas concert weeks in advance and I strove to rehearse until mine was letter perfect. There were the geese and ducks to butcher and dress, and new feather ticks to be made. My mother let me help with cookies and other special treats in the kitchen. My father would take me to the bottom of the farm fields to cut a tree to put in the house, where we all could take part in decorating it with simple homemade ornaments.

Then, of course, there was the anticipation of Santa's visit. It didn't matter that what he left was not elaborate; it was always priceless in my eyes. There would be a colouring book and crayons, and a book to read. My eyes lit up with delight at the new clothing my aunt had made and the hard candy from my uncle who managed the Brace, McKay & Co. store in Summerside. My mother, sparing what sugar she could, would make sweet brown fudge. What more could a child want?

So I was eager for Christmas 1929. When I woke up on the morning of Christmas Eve, the school concert was over, the tree was decorated, though still bare underneath, and there were good smells coming from the kitchen. The anticipation rose in my stomach as I thought of what just one more sleep would bring. I scurried to dress and head downstairs to get my chores done because I wanted nothing to upset the generous mood of Santa Claus.

What a surprise when I walked into the kitchen: there sat my Grandmother MacAusland! I assumed she had come for Christmas, but my feeling of delight quickly turned to disbelief. My parents, who were also in the kitchen, proceeded to tell me I would be leaving home for Christmas; I was to pack a bag for a visit with my Aunt Margaret and Uncle Loman in the village of St. Eleanors. And I was to be quick about it, for Father had the horse hitched to the sleigh and was ready to be off.

What was this? Oh, I liked my aunt and uncle well enough, but I certainly did not want to spend Christmas with them on my own.

However, I did not create a scene or even give voice to the questions racing through my mind. This was an era when children were to be seen and not heard. I quietly sat beside my father in the sleigh as the little mare, step by step, transported us along the New Road from Southwest to Miscouche and then along the Cannon Road to St. Eleanors. My mind worked feverishly to come up with the reason why I was being banned from home for Christmas. Obviously it was about me, for my twenty-month-old brother was not going anywhere.

I thought and thought…then I thought even harder, trying to come up with an answer. I had been diligent about my chores. I was obedient to my mother and father, other than with the horse—could they have smelled him on me? Or maybe they had discovered that on occasion I sneaked across the road to play with the neighbour children when I was expected to be working. But those two rules were the only ones I had broken. Surely they were not serious enough for me to be sent away at Christmastime?

With my mind still working at top speed, I searched for more reasons for this unexpected trip: I didn't tease my brother, the cat, or the dog, and most importantly I had not risked the sin of doing homework on a Sunday. So why was this happening? The only answer that made any sense to me was that with the unexpected arrival of Grandmother MacAusland, there was no time to bother with me. How would Santa now know where to find me? More importantly, would he still want to find me?

Eventually, we arrived at Aunt Margaret and Uncle Loman's in St. Eleanors. The Adams farm was tucked neatly between the Tanton Farm and the Darby Farm, names I had heard associated with the United Empire Loyalists and the American Revolution. My aunt and uncle's house was a beautiful old home with twelve-foot ceilings and filled with fancy furniture. The most amazing things in the house, to my eyes, were a fireplace and running water provided by a cistern in the cellar.

Aunt Margaret kept the place like a museum. When she got up in the morning, regardless of the weather, she threw open a window at the back of the house and the door at the front of the house to let the wind blow through and then she began to clean. Since my Aunt Margaret, Mother's older sister, made her own money as a tailor, her house held objects my mother could only dream about. She even had a splendid fur coat.

Uncle Loman, originally of Port Hill, was a cheese maker as well as a farmer. He had a fine herd of cattle and bottled and sold milk by the quart right from his farm. He was considered very successful, a fact proven by his ownership of one of the first cars in the area. Uncle Loman and Aunt Margaret had one daughter, Belle, who had a job teaching school down east in Fortune. She was home for Christmas and all three of them seemed strict and very concerned about manners.

Father left me with the instructions that I was to behave myself and cause no trouble. He didn't need to worry. If I got into trouble it certainly would not have been intentional. The Adams family did their best to make me feel at home—at least, the best you can do without telling a child anything about what is happening. Somehow I slept that night and Santa Claus did find me, although my memory of what he brought is unclear. I do know with certainty it would not have been a doll, for there was no money for dolls.

On Christmas morning, Aunt Margaret informed me they were having special guests for Christmas dinner. Summerside's police officer, James Sullivan, and his wife, Margaret, were invited, and I was to be on my best behaviour. My heart dropped to my stomach. I had met Officer Sullivan before. He wasn't very tall, but he had a large paunch. That, combined with his gruff voice and police uniform, meant I was terrified of him.

When they arrived, Mrs. Sullivan was wearing a beautiful dress and white gloves, something I had never seen before. Aunt Margaret certainly put on a show with the table setting. It was beautiful and the food was delicious for she was an excellent cook. We had duck and a large moist capon with all the trimmings. I did them proud: I sat up straight and used my best table manners, and made it successfully through the meal with no blunders, but sadly no enjoyment either.

They took me to the Christmas service at St. John's Anglican Church just down the road. Aunt Margaret gave me a penny for the collection. I was mortified, for at home I always was given a nickel. I could not imagine placing only a penny in the collection plate when it was passed, but that is what I did.

By evening I was not a happy girl. I sat looking out the window wondering what was happening at home and when Father would come back for me. Boxing Day passed the same way. Just when it seemed there was no hope, I heard the horse and sleigh in the yard. There was Father, stomping the snow from his boots at the door and Uncle Loman inviting him inside. Suddenly they were all laughing, shaking hands, and clapping each other on the back as though something exciting had happened. Father said to me, "Vera, you have a new brother at home. Are you ready to go see him?"

The sleigh ride home seemed to take forever. My father had not even brought the sleigh to a stop in the yard before I jumped out and rushed into the house. When I laid eyes on my baby brother, Wendell, the story of the birth of Christ took on a new meaning. I suddenly understood what the shepherds must have felt on that night so long ago. I smiled at the tiny bundle. He was much better than a doll!

Wendell was the Christmas gift that kept giving. He livened up all of our lives, for there was nothing he did not get into or try. I had him in my life for seventy-six Christmases, until a heart attack claimed him one beautiful September evening in 2006. He lives on in my heart and in my memory, as the gift that both ruined and made the Christmas of 1929.

The Unforgettable Christmas

(1931)

THE NARRATOR OF THIS STORY IS MY MOTHER, GLEN MACARTHUR CAMPBELL. GROWING UP I KNEW VERY FEW DETAILS OF THIS EVENT IN HER LIFE. IT WAS JUST A FACT AND NEVER DISCUSSED. BUT IN 2010, I DECIDED IT WAS TIME I KNEW THE WHOLE STORY.

Lord willing, 2010 will be my eighty-third Christmas. There are a lot of memories of Christmases past floating about in my head. Most of them, when recalled, are little clips that have no clear title identifying them as the Christmas of a certain year. But there is one Christmas that is firmly imprinted upon my memory. It is the Christmas I was three and one half years. Ah! You're thinking *here comes a tall tale*. But I speak the truth. Although I was young, it was an unforgettable Christmas.

My memories do not begin on December 25 or even the evening before, but a full two weeks prior to the much-anticipated day. It was 1931 and I had not a care in the world other than to make sure my days were filled with the work of children—play. I was the second daughter and final child of Jessie and Gordon MacArthur. My parents were a couple that, for the times, had married late. My father was a veteran of the First World War and had a passion for history and politics. But, having no avenue to pursue either subject, he farmed a hundred-acre farm in Arlington, Prince Edward Island. My mother was the oldest of seven sisters and it could be said she had helped raise a family before she even had her own children. She was a woman I would come to admire for her talent at making something from nothing. I remember her sitting at her sewing machine hour after hour creating beautiful clothing for those who could afford the services of a seamstress. And for those who could not, she still created.

My sister, Jean, was older by three years and we were as different as day and night. She was a proper girl who did all the things little girls ought to. I, on the other hand, was described as a strong-willed, independent, and adventurous girl who sought out trouble at every turn. In September 1931, Jean began to attend the one-room schoolhouse about a mile up the road. No doubt my mother felt the greatest impact of this, for I was constantly at her for one thing or another. What I demanded most was to be let outside to play, where I was content for hours at a time. That was a constant worry for my mother because the farmyard was nestled in a valley between two fast-flowing streams I was fascinated with. And then of course there were the barns and the animals. Mother never worried about letting Jean and I out to play together because she knew Jean would follow her instructions and would make sure I did the same. When I went out alone she had to constantly interrupt her work in the house or barn to check on me.

The day that sticks in my memory was sunny and mild. There was just enough snow on the ground for the horses and sleighs to travel but not enough to impede the few cars that might go by at the top of the very long lane. Jean was at school, my father was at work somewhere outside, and my mother was busy trying to finish Christmas sewing orders. I was content to spend the morning in the house, playing with a few simple toys on the floor of the kitchen. After the noon meal, however, I demanded to go outside to play with the sleigh I had received the previous Christmas. I was told to wait for Jean, but that was not to my liking and I kicked up such a commotion that I eventually wore my mother down. She finally said the words I wanted to hear: "Go get your outdoor clothing."

I ran to the coat hook behind the kitchen range and took down my clothing and boots. I remember as though it was yesterday what I was dressed in that day. My mother made everything I wore and I was proud of my outfits. My little dress was grey wool trimmed with red, and my coat was cut down from an old adult coat. Of course she had knitted the mittens, hat, and scarf I wore, as well as the heavy woollen stockings. Mother pulled the leggings on over my leather shoes and full-length tights and then put my black overboots on top. Next came the coat buttoned from top to bottom, followed by the hat, the scarf, and—finally!—the mittens.

The whole time she was dressing me she was telling me to stay away from the streams and not to dare go near the horse stable. It annoyed me that she always reminded me about the horse stable for it was the one place I never did go; in truth, the large animals frightened me. My father had three horses. There was the long-legged, bad-tempered Archie who liked to dance around and make a lot of noise; the little mare, Nellie, who carried the majority of the workload; and Nellie's colt, Harry, born the previous spring. In my mind he was all legs and never stood still. If Father did take me near him, the playful animal would nudge me with his head and try to knock me down.

When I got outside the door I was happy to find such a beautiful day. I ran for my sleigh and set out to play. My only question was where to go first, and the answer was always the same. Pulling the sleigh behind me, I headed through the barnyard to the treeline where two fox pens were located. Only one had an occupant—an old red fox I enjoyed visiting (and was certain she was equally pleased with my company). I stood close enough to admire every detail of her sleek body but far enough away that my fingers couldn't be bitten. As usual, Mrs. Fox was a great listener and we had a delightful conversation. I was interrupted during one of my tales by the sound of a horse and sleigh coming down the lane. It turned into the farmyard and made its way to the horse barn.

I jumped up, eager to identify who it was, and was filled with excitement when I recognized my Uncle Herb and his son, Elmer. Elmer was thirteen and, in my mind, a most impressive young man. I wanted badly to see him, but took the time to say a proper goodbye to Mrs. Fox before I grasped the rope of my sleigh and headed for the barn. It was a lengthy trip for short legs, and before I was even halfway there, they had the horse unhitched from the sleigh and were entering the horse stable. They hadn't even noticed me. I stopped in my tracks, utterly disappointed. I would have to wait for them to come back out in order to see Elmer. I brightened when I remembered it would only be a moment—they would put Uncle Herb's cranky little mare in a stall and come back out to find my father.

Unbeknownst to me, my father was in the horse stable waiting for Uncle Herb to help him trim the mare's hoofs. Elmer had taken the day off school to come along on the errand. I waited patiently at first and then impatiently for them to emerge. I walked around and around pulling my sleigh and even coasted down the small hill by the lane a few times but always with an eye to the stable door. I also kept my eye on the house door and kitchen window from which I knew my mother was checking my whereabouts every few minutes. But curiosity was getting the better of me. Hauling my sleigh behind me I edged closer and closer to the door, which was slightly ajar. Glancing back to the house to make certain my mother was not watching, I slipped inside the stable and surveyed my surroundings.

The colt was roaming freely in the box stall and, like me, was taking everything in. Nellie and Archie were tied in their stalls with their back ends to the walkway. Uncle Herb's horse was tied in the empty stall next to Harry. She was known to have a mind of her own—she only moved when she wanted to and balked when she didn't. Uncle Herb was just about finished putting the harness on her. My father and Elmer stood with their backs to me watching him at work. None of them saw me enter the stable or sensed my presence. I moved to stand directly behind my father. Still he remained unaware of me as he conversed with his brother.

His task completed, Uncle Herb started to back the mare out of her stall into the walkway. She was resisting his command when Harry, the colt, leaned over the partition and bit her flank. She let out a whinny and kicked her back leg out in defense. The leg came straight for my father's knee and he instinctively jumped aside to escape the blow. The hoof smashed into the left side of my small face and the impact knocked me backwards, still conscious, onto the hard floor.

When my father turned and saw me lying there, fear filled his body. My nose remained attached to my face only by a thread of skin. He didn't utter a word; he simply scooped me up and began to run for the house. Cradled in his arms I felt safe and repeated, "I want to sleep with you guys tonight" over and over again. When he burst into the kitchen, my mother was able to keep her wits about her and grabbed a large quilt in which she gently wrapped me. She instinctively began to rock me to try and keep shock from setting in. Uncle Herb and Elmer were close behind my father and they hurriedly discussed what to do next. The nearest hospital was in Summerside, eighteen miles away. Our family went there once a year on the train just before Christmas. It seemed imperative that I be taken to town, but the question was how to accomplish it. The train left from Northam early every morning and the few local farmers who owned cars had likely put them into winter storage.

It was decided that Uncle Herb would go to Tyne Valley, three miles away, to ask the doctor there to come to the house. But Dr. Stewart's territory covered many miles and there was no way of knowing how quickly we could find him. Still, Uncle Herb had to try. In the meantime, my father knew he couldn't just sit and wait for word. He went down the road to look for the two farmers in Arlington who owned automobiles. At the homes of Beecher Dennis and Clarence Phillips the story was the same: they had taken the wheels off their cars and they were up on blocks for the winter. There was only one chance left: Neil McLellan's farm in Grand River, several miles away. This time my father was in luck: Mr. McLellan's car was still operational and he was willing to make the journey.

During the time my father and Uncle Herb were out seeking assistance, Elmer had been sent across the fields to the next farm to get my Grandmother Cameron and then to the school to collect my sister Jean. When they arrived, they sat quietly with me in the kitchen while we waited for my father to return. I had no idea of the turmoil or the guilt that was going through my mother's mind as she held me in her arms. When my father arrived with Mr. McLellan, not a moment was wasted getting my mother and me into the vehicle. If there was a silver lining to be found in the situation it was that the road was still passable for automobiles. It was a fairly smooth ride although my injured face responded painfully to every rut in the road. It took ninety minutes to cover the eighteen miles and I am sure I only made it more difficult for the adults with my constantly asking "How much longer?"

When we finally arrived at the Prince County Hospital on Central Street, my father carried me inside and placed me on the examining table. I had never seen such a big building or experienced such strange smells. Fear began to rise until I recognized the person who greeted us. My Aunt Edith, Mother's sister, was a night nurse supervisor at the hospital. Her touch reassured me. That feeling only lasted until the nurses started to cut my clothes off. I got angry and ordered them not to cut my good dress Mother had just made. They didn't listen. I was stripped and put into a hospital gown.

Then Dr. Sinclair, who I remember as a middle-aged man with glasses, arrived to examine me—another new experience. He told my parents that while my eye was still intact, "the sight had run out of it." He would fix my nose as best he could.

And that is just what he did. He sewed it back into place with such fine delicate stitches that in later years you'd be hard-pressed to see a scar. The drain he placed in it ensured no infection ever set in. But I wasn't necessarily appreciative of his work. In the following days when he visited me in my hospital bed, I greeted him with, "Touch me and I'll bite you. Goddammit, I'll bite you." My poor Presbyterian mother was mortified. I, on the other hand, gave not a moment's grief to the young Dr. Simpson when he did rounds.

The only setback during my lengthy hospital stay was my reaction to the pain medication. Instead of falling into a deep slumber that would allow my body to heal, I would thrash about and talk in my sleep. It was disconcerting to the poor nurses, who thought I was prophesying. My words were likely the result of the many hours I had spent listening to my Grandmother Cameron read from a picture Bible. Under the influence of drugs, I would recite such verses as "Everyone who hears these words of mine and puts them into practice is like a wise man who built his house on the rock" and "The rain came down, the streams rose, and the winds blew and beat against the house, yet it did not fall because it had its foundation on the rock." I continued the scripture: "Everyone who hears these words of mine and does not put them into practice is like a foolish man who built his house on sand. The rain came down, the streams rose, and the winds blew and beat against that house, and it fell with a great crash." They were heavy words indeed for a three-and-a-half-year-old girl.

I grew stronger day by day. Dr. Sinclair visited me regularly and was always kind, gentle, and tolerant of my moods. My mother stayed in Summerside and came each day to sit with me. I was unaware that Christmas was drawing nearer, and she was not at home to make preparations. This chore had fallen to Grandmother Cameron and my father. Jean felt the loss of our mother especially. She missed her during the preparations for the school concert, the making of special treats like sugar cookies, and the countdown of days to the special feast at our grandparents'.

Slowly, little signs appeared around the hospital to signal that Christmas was coming. A few simple decorations adorned the walls and I heard staff talking about the day growing near. My mother said little about it. She knew we wouldn't be home for Christmas, but she gave no indication of disappointment.

There was no mention of Santa because we had not yet been introduced to the custom, nor was there any reference to the few simple gifts I would have received at home by my breakfast plate on Christmas morning.

As the days passed, I heard the beautiful tones of large bells for the first time in my life. My mother said they were in the steeple of St. Paul's Church down the street. I thought that sound was the most amazing thing.

I woke to them on Christmas morning in the Prince County Hospital. All of the nurses wished me Merry Christmas and I thought it was wonderful that they were in an extra good mood that morning.

As I lay in bed looking about with my one good eye, Dr. Sinclair came into my room. He stood by my bed and held out a box and said, "Here is a little gift for you, Glen." I reached out my small hands and took the box from him. I lifted the lid and gasped with amazement at what was inside: a porcelain doll the size a child could hold in her arms. She had lovely brown hair and was dressed in a little white coat and hat with leather boots on her feet. I had never seen nor held anything like her before. I was in such awe that I don't believe I even said thank you to Dr. Sinclair. I did not even notice him leave the room. I am sure I did receive other gifts that Christmas, but I only remember the doll. In later years when Santa became a part of my Christmas tradition, I imagined him to be Dr. Sinclair.

A week after Christmas, I travelled home with my mother on the train to Northam. My father met us at the station with the horse and sleigh and we continued on to our home in Arlington.

During the trip I cradled my precious doll in my arms. I had named her Diane. I never played with her very much other than to dress and undress her, for my mother would say, "Now remember, Dr. Sinclair gave her to you. Don't you tear her apart." For years she sat in an honoured place on a shelf in my room where I would admire her as I drifted off to sleep at night. She was my silent and steadfast companion as I grew into womanhood.

And so it was my treasured porcelain doll, rather than a lost eye, that became the strongest memory of an unforgettable Christmas.

The Christmas Spirit of 1934

AS A CHILD I OFTEN HEARD MY MOTHER SPEAK OF GROW-
ING UP DURING THE GREAT DEPRESSION AND THE SECOND
WORLD WAR. ALTHOUGH MONEY WAS TIGHT, THE LOVE OF
FAMILY PROTECTED HER AND HER SISTER FROM MUCH OF THE
HARSHNESS OF THE TIME.

In 1934, Canada was in the midst of an economic depression. But for two young girls in rural Prince Edward Island, that was irrelevant—Christmas was coming and Glen, age six, and Jean, age nine, were excited. In their minds, money didn't matter because the special day would mark Christ's birth and it was Santa Claus who did the gift giving. Mother was certain that Santa would also be experiencing the Great Depression, but Glen and Jean were equally sure he wouldn't. They had heard the stories of Santa and his workshop full of elves busily making toys. Santa was magical and the Depression couldn't affect magic.

By some standards, Santa hadn't brought much in the past years. There had been an orange in the toe of the sock, barley suckers and hard candy, a toy, and a wonderful book that Father and Mother read to them over and over. In the eyes of the two small girls, Santa was the most generous of men, and his gifts were treasures to behold. This year, considering they had been good and nice, things should be no different.

In the weeks leading up to Christmas, the MacArthur household was filled with quiet excitement. Glen and Jean practiced their parts for the school Christmas concert and trimmed the house with strings of cranberry and popcorn. They didn't have a Christmas tree in the parlour like some of their school-mates even though their farm had a large woodlot. Father thought it a senseless practice to cut down a perfectly good tree to stand in the house for just a few days, but he did cut a few evergreen boughs to add colour and fragrance to the house. That small bit of decoration, mixed with the smell of Mother's Christmas sugar cookies, mincemeat pies, and plum pudding, gave the sense that Christmas was near.

Glen and Jean wrote their letters to Santa from their home in Arlington and travelled by horse and sleigh with their father to the railway station in Northam to send them on the train. Father assured them the Island train would connect with the one travelling to the North Pole.

In their letters, the girls had asked for nothing. They inquired after Santa's health and that of Mrs. Claus and the elves, and questioned if the Depression was hurting them the same way it was hurting others. They explained that they had been very good throughout the year and they hoped he could find his way to their home between the two brooks in Arlington. The choice of a present they would leave up to Santa, although each child had her own secret dream.

Mother's Christmas gift for both girls was new clothing. She was a seamstress, and said not even the Great Depression could take that away. She brought an old red dress, long out of fashion, down from the attic. She washed it and carefully took apart the seams, and had enough material to make matching skirts and vests for Glen and Jean. As they stood to be fitted in the middle of the old kitchen, they were proud. They felt as though they were trying on the finest clothing in Holman's Department Store in Summerside. (They had visited the store once when they had travelled to town by train.)

As Christmas crept closer, Glen and Jean checked the freshly fallen snow for reindeer tracks. Mother told them Santa sent an elf out each night during the week before Christmas to see if the girls were being good. Of course, their chores (clearing the table, filling the wood box) were done cheerfully, but the girls wanted proof and hoofprints would be ideal. They checked the roadway each morning as they walked to school but couldn't tell the difference between horse hooves and reindeer hooves. It proved most frustrating.

One Christmas tradition the girls didn't look forward to was the killing of the Christmas geese. Father raised the beautiful white and grey birds for the Christmas market as ready cash for the family. A plump goose was the favourite of many people for Christmas dinner. Since the geese had to be fresh when delivered, they could only be killed a few days before Christmas and everyone in the family was called upon to help.

The girls had to pluck the feathers from the headless birds as they hung from the ceiling in the killing shed. The feathers came out easily from the still-warm flesh. Plucking was tiring work for their small arms, but the girls knew that for many households, Christmas dinner meant a goose on the table. They stuffed the feathers into burlap bags—Mother would clean them and make fresh ticks and pillows for their beds. As they worked, they thought about the little yellow goslings they had fed over the summer and autumn and watched grow into elegant young geese. It was hard to say goodbye, but as farm children they understood the cycle of life. Next spring there would be new little yellow goslings that would need their tender care.

Finally, Christmas Eve day arrived, and Glen and Jean were so full of energy their mother sent them outside to play. They hauled their sleds up the hill by the front brook and sledded down toward the open trickle of water. The adventure was in seeing how close to the brook they could come without getting wet. Up and down the hill they went, the runners barely marking the crispness of the snow. Soon, their cheeks were red from exertion and the brisk December air.

As they climbed the hill once again, the girls saw a horse and sleigh turn into the laneway of their farm and begin its descent to the hollow. Who could be coming to visit the day before Christmas? As the sleigh drew closer, the girls let out a whoop as they recognized their Aunt Edith. When she climbed out, the girls raced into her open arms and plied her with questions about where she had come from and whether she was staying.

Aunt Edith was Mother's unmarried sister and a nurse at the hospital in Summerside. She was like a goddess in the girls' eyes: she was tall, slim, and even at their young age they could sense her inner strength. Aunt Edith seemed to take command of a situation and yet her heart was gentle. She always had time for the girls and brought them special little treats. In response to their questions there was a firm yes: she was staying for Christmas and did they have her bed made up?

When Father came out of the barn to take the horse to the stable, the girls carried Aunt Edith's bag to the house. They noted that it seemed heavier than usual but once inside, Aunt Edith didn't open it, much to their disappointment. Having their aunt in the house made the day speed by. She played a board game with them, read them a book, and told them about the little girl she was nursing at the hospital. Before they knew it, supper was over and it was time to get ready for bed.

They had to prepare a snack for Santa. Glen and Jean went down into the cold cellar and picked out a round, plump turnip from the vegetable pile. Back in the kitchen, they cut the top from the turnip and laid out a spoon so Santa could scrape off the sweet yellow pulp. Turnip was a common Depression-era lunch in Arlington and the girls were sure Santa and his reindeer would enjoy it.

Mother tucked the girls into bed and Aunt Edith laid down to tell them a story about how Santa was on his annual journey....

In the wink of an eye, the light of morning was pouring into the bedroom and Jean woke Glen with yells of, "Get up, get up! It's Christmas morning!" They raced down to the kitchen in their pyjamas and found the fire burning brightly and the table set for breakfast. Beside each place setting was one gift wrapped in brown paper and a small bulging stocking at the girls' places.

Shaking with excitement, they slipped into their chairs and Father agreed, just this once, that the parcels could be opened before the porridge was served. Glen, being the youngest, went first. Her stocking was heavy to lift into her lap. Slowly, she reached inside and felt something soft. It was a pair of red mittens, followed by a red hat, barley candy, and an orange. But still there was something in the toe. Glen pulled out the prettiest silver locket she had ever seen. How could Santa have known that after having seen Muriel MacLean's locket, she had dreamed of owning something just as beautiful? She shook her head—Santa was magical.

Jean's stocking contained blue mittens, a blue hat, barley candy, and an orange. Tucked in the toe was a silver ring that fit her finger perfectly. She exclaimed loudly, "See Momma, I told you the Depression wasn't hurting Santa!" Both girls missed the look exchanged by the three adults.

Next, the family tore into their brown paper packages. Jean and Glen received one book each. Father's parcel held warm knitted socks, Mother's a doily, and Aunt Edith's contained red mittens and a blue hat to match those of Glen and Jean. In the midst of hardship, it was a Christmas of plenty. Even the Great Depression was unable to destroy the magic of Santa Claus.

Plum Pudding Christmas

(1935)

Jean MacArthur Yeo recounted this story in November 2011 as she prepared for her first Christmas in a nursing home. She was struggling with being a patient there due to her difficulty walking, and the change of not celebrating Christmas in her own home. She was also facing her second Christmas without her husband of sixty years, Jack. As we began to talk of her childhood Christmases, concerns and limitations fell away as she travelled back in time to her Grandma's kitchen.

E ven before I opened my eyes I felt the excitement that comes from anticipation. It was Christmas Eve morning and there was much to be done to prepare for Christmas Day. I felt the cold of the unheated bedroom on my face, the only body part not covered by Mother's heavy quilts. I wanted to burrow deeper into the fresh feather tick she had placed on the bed the previous night. It had been made from the feathers of geese and ducks to be served for Christmas dinner throughout the county. For a moment, I felt sad: I would never again hear their honks as they gathered round the feed bucket when I brought them dinner. But as a farm child, I understood the cycle of life. I also knew this was not the day to give in to my desire to linger because Grandma would be waiting for me.

As the oldest female grandchild on my mother's side, I was going to help my grandmother with the Christmas feast preparations for her large family. It was a wonderful privilege for a ten-year-old girl and I took it seriously. After all, I was a serious child. I suppose it came from being the eldest of two. Then again, maybe it came from having been named Jean Elfinella when I was born in 1925. It would take a serious child to be able to handle a name such as Elfinella, which my father, a voracious reader, had come across in a book.

I quickly dressed in the biting cold of my bedroom before running down the stairs to the warmth of the kitchen. My sister, Glen, was nowhere to be seen and I was secretly glad for I wanted to go to Grandma's house on my own. Even though Glen was three years younger than I, we were good friends—but things hadn't started off that way. When she was born on a fine day in June 1928, I was less than impressed and ran from the house into the fields to hide in order to show my displeasure. But with time, and some attitude adjustment on my part, we became friends. Over the years, we sourced out whatever trouble there was to be found on our farm and in the small community of

Arlington. Even so, I didn't want to share this special Christmas Eve day at our grandmother's with her.

I swiftly ate the oatmeal porridge sprinkled with dark brown sugar Mother set before me. I donned my outdoor clothing and struck out across the field to the farm of my grandparents, John and Margaret Cameron. It was truly a wonderful thing to be able to cross the field of my father's farm, slip under the wire fence, and break through the treeline at my grandfather's land. I stood for a moment looking at the farmhouse and buildings nestled in the hollow between two streams. With the smoke curling up from the house chimney and the roofs lightly covered with snow glistening in the sunshine, it looked like a Christmas card.

I began to run across the stubble field that was all that separated me from the farmstead. Grandfather Cameron was proud of his Arlington farm. He was known for his skills as a farmer who raised fine horses and cattle and harvested prosperous crops. His brother Allan, a carpenter who had never married, was part of the household and made sure the buildings stayed in fine shape.

My grandparents had raised a family of seven girls from the bounty of the farm. My mother, Jessie, whom Great Uncle Allan had named after a former girlfriend, was the eldest and they were happy to have her raising her family on the farm next door. My father had been able to purchase it with the help of the War Veterans Board after returning from active service in the First World War. Glen and I, along with all the cousins, could always count on a warm welcome at our grandparents' home.

The moment I pushed open the door of the old farmhouse, I felt the warmth of the kitchen range and breathed in the smell of wood stacked high in the woodbox. The smell of the fresh Christmas tree, already set up and decorated, wafted from the parlour. I saw my grandmother's welcoming smile and she told me to quickly hang my coat and wash my hands—we had plum pudding to make.

We moved into the small pantry off the kitchen. This was a room I truly loved for it was the centre of Grandma's wonderful culinary creations. A window that looked out over the orchard poured bright winter light into the room. The apple trees, with their harvest stored in the root cellar, stood devoid of leaves though still majestic in winter sleep. One wall of the pantry housed the short extension of cupboards that held all of Grandma's kitchen utensils and dishes other than her finest, which were kept in a cabinet in the dining room. The other wall housed open shelves for pots, pans, cookie sheets, earthenware bowls, and tins and crocks filled with cooking and baking ingredients. The large wooden flour barrel dominated the open corner. The work surface was an oak wooden table that retained its shine despite the countless batches of bread, pie crusts, biscuits, and cookies that had been kneaded, rolled out, and shaped on it.

Grandma placed an earthenware bowl on the table and carefully opened the large tin can used to store the fruit needed for the pudding. The large, sticky Lexia raisins were as precious as gold and when mixed with citrus peels, were savoured in the Christmas feast. She reverently placed them in the bowl, sprinkled them with flour, and let me separate with my fingers the pieces of fruit and coat them with flour so they would not sink to the bottom of the pudding, but spread evenly throughout the mixture. When the job was done and the fruit set aside, I, with her approval, licked my sticky fingers clean before washing them in preparation for the next step.

In her largest earthenware bowl my grandmother began mixing the batter, measuring with her eye the necessary amount of dry and liquid ingredients. First was pig tallow, the fat rendered when a pig raised over the summer was butchered in late fall and salted down. She removed it from a tin and placed it in the bowl. I gently creamed it against the sides and bottom with a wooden spoon. Once smooth, we stirred in dark brown sugar, and I was allowed to dip in my finger and scoop out a small taste before we added the brown farm eggs, collected that very morning from the henhouse, into the creamy mixture. Then came the thick molasses out of the glass keg that had been filled at the store in Tyne Valley, followed by milk soured with baking soda.

In a second bowl we prepared the dry ingredients. I was allowed to sift the flour (ground at the mill from the fall wheat harvest) through the silver-coloured sifter. I held it low into the bowl as I turned the handle to keep the fine flour dust from drifting onto the work table. Grandma opened her spice tins and the air filled with the heavenly smell of cinnamon, allspice, and nutmeg, which we carefully stirred into the flour. Next, we combined the dry ingredients with the wet, and finally folded in the fruit. The batter was now so thick and heavy my grandmother had to do the final stir.

She had sewn a long, narrow pudding bag from the cotton material of a flour bag. She turned it inside out, wet it with water, and then coated it with flour. Then, turning it right side out again, we spooned in the pudding batter until the bag was three-quarters full. Ever so carefully, I helped Grandma tie the bag tightly shut with string to prevent any water from entering as the pudding steamed. Once again, I licked the bowl clean.

Waiting on the kitchen stove was the large roaster half-filled with boiling water. I watched as my grandmother carefully removed the roaster cover and placed in the bag of pudding to steam. Two hours on one side and two hours on the other side is a long time to wait for a pudding to cook. We had to keep the fire hot and add new water as it evaporated.

But the time was not idle—there was more to do in the pantry with the making of mince tarts and sugar cookies. When my grandmother cut out the cookies and laid them on the cookie sheet, I placed a raisin in the centre of each and sprinkled them lightly with large chunks of granulated sugar. Soon the air filled with the mouth-watering smells of Christmas baking.

We prepared the dressing for the goose from stale bread. We tore the slices into small chunks until the large bowls were filled to the brim, and then added cold mashed potatoes, chopped onions that always made my eyes water, homemade butter, salt, pepper, and best of all: summer savoury from Grandma's garden. We brought up the vegetables from the root cellar: round white potatoes, long slender carrots, large firm turnips, and stubby parsnips. We peeled and chopped until the pots were filled. To ensure the vegetables stayed fresh until cooking, we covered them in cold water sprinkled with salt.

When the plum pudding was finally cooked, my grandmother carefully removed it from the boiling water and placed it on a cooling rack. We busied ourselves with other chores while we waited for it to cool so we could remove it from the bag. That was an art in itself, the procedure having to be done very carefully in order to remove the pudding intact. I watched with bated breath as my grandmother gently peeled back the pudding bag to reveal, inch by inch, the dark brown pudding. Once it was freed from the bag, she wrapped it in cheesecloth and gently placed it in a tin for Christmas Day.

Before I knew it, the magical day had passed and my mother had come to take me home. As we walked across the snow-covered fields by the light of the moon, I kept glancing into the sky hoping for a glimpse of Santa and his reindeer. All I saw were the bright stars of the constellations. In my vivid imagination they were winking at me as though they knew where he could be found. Once home, I wasted no time making preparations for bed. I knew the faster I fell asleep, the quicker the dawn of Christmas would be ushered in.

When morning arrived there was no question about lingering in bed. Glen and I bolted down the stairs to discover Christmas socks and gifts wrapped in brown paper sitting beside our breakfast plates. Each sock held an orange, ribbon candy, and some barley animal candy. We each received a pull horse, both of them yellow with tails and manes, standing on a platform with red wheels that allowed them to be pulled about using the reins of the bridle. I knew there were hours of imaginative play ahead for us. The best gift of all was a new outfit my mother had sewn that I planned to wear to the family Christmas dinner.

Impatient though I was to get to my grandparents' home, I had to wait for the rest of the family. After we opened our gifts, we ate breakfast. Then Father went out to do the farm chores while Glen and I helped Mother wash the dishes and straighten the house. Finally we could dress in our best clothing and make our way on foot across the fields. Glen and I raced ahead of our parents to see which of the aunts, uncles, and cousins had arrived or were making their way down the long lane.

Aunt Cora and Uncle Lorne came by horse and sleigh from Birch Hill, and Uncle Willie and Aunt Margaret came from Riverside. Uncle Clarence and Aunt Olive, who lived on the upper road, drove down in their car. There were also the maiden aunts in their late teens, Blanche and Dorothy, who had arrived home from work on Christmas Eve. Aunt Edith, a nursing night-supervisor at Prince County Hospital, came all the way from Summerside and brought gifts for the children. Best of all were my young cousins—Ronnie, Allan, Hughie, Duncan, Donald, and Edna.

Greetings of "Merry Christmas!" rang out as soon as we opened the door of the house. The smell coming from the kitchen was heavenly. Grandma had made fresh bread and biscuits long before the sun came up, and the goose had occupied the oven for hours. The kitchen was toasty warm and the base burner in the hallway was radiating heat into the dining room and parlour.

The men and children went off to admire the tree in the parlour while the women set about preparing the Christmas feast. The vegetables were put to boil on top of the wood stove, and the table in the dining room was set with all of Grandma's dishes—the good set that usually rested in the china cabinet supplemented by the everyday ones. Even though every last dish and piece of silverware was out, there was only enough seating and dishes for the adults. The children were expected to wait for a second setting. Though our stomachs may have rumbled, we didn't complain; we had plenty to occupy us by gathering round and playing with our Christmas gifts.

When the adults were done, they rose and cooked fresh vegetables, washed the dishes, and reset the dining room table for the children's feast. And what a feast it was. Delicious roasted goose, mounds of stuffing, carrots, turnips, parsnips, and potatoes covered in gravy, pickled beets, and mustard pickles. Not to mention the fresh bread and biscuits slathered with Grandma's homemade butter. The steaming plates were served to us, seated, just as the adults had been, around the dining room table. After the main course, we somehow found room for plum pudding covered in brown sugar sauce, sugar cookies, and mince tarts, which we washed down with cups of tea.

When at last we had our fill, everyone helped clear the table and wash and put away the dishes. Then we all gathered in the parlour for an evening of storytelling and song. The

Cameron family were music lovers and an old organ held a prominent place in the room. However, on that Christmas night, we sang ballads that were much loved in the day. Uncle Lorne took a pint from his pocket and passed it around to the men. He made sure Father had a few sips of the toddy, for then he could be coaxed to sing on his own. We all called for him to sing a song called "The Chippewa Stream," which he rendered in his deep baritone voice.

As I went a-walking one evening in June
A-viewing the roses—they were in full bloom—
I met a pretty fair maid as I passed along;
She was washing some linens by the Chippewa Stream

I went up beside her and I made a low bow
And what I said to her I'll tell to you now:
"It's been twelve months or better my mind's been on thee
And it's now we'll get married if you will agree."

"O to marry, to marry, kind sir, I'm too young.
Besides all you young men have a false flattering tongue!
How cross my mother and my father would be
if I was to wed with a rover like thee."

He turned around quickly, knowing well what to say:
"I wish you a good man, a good man I pray.
The sky it looks heavy, I think we'll have rain."
So they shook hands and parted on the Chippewa Stream.

"O come back, love, come back, you've quite won my heart.
It is now we'll get married and never depart.
'Tis now we'll get married and happy I'll be,
and live happy together 'till the day we do die."

"O the last words you spoke, love, was far out of tune.
O the last words you spoke, love, I've quite changed my mind.
I think it's far better for single to remain
Than to court some pretty fair maid on the Chippewa Stream."

(FROM *BALLADS AND SEA SONGS FROM NOVA SCOTIA*
BY W. ROY MACKENZIE)

Adult and child alike listened intently to Father's every word, spellbound by his deep voice and thoughts of the perils of love and courtship. Uncle Lorne passed the toddy again, and the more Uncle Clarence refused a sip, the more Uncle Lorne enjoyed the challenge of trying to persuade him to take just one before calling for another song or story. And so the evening passed with the warmth and comfort of family gathered in the old farmhouse nestled in the hollow.

All too soon it was time to go home.

I felt content as we walked back across the fields to our house. In my young mind, I never imagined Christmas to be any different than the one just celebrated. But change, the only constant in life, was on the horizon. The Great Depression was taking its toll and the private storekeeper who held the mortgage on my grandparents' farm called for the outstanding balance.

Whether the timing was legitimate or opportunistic, the blow to my grandparents was heart-wrenching. After many years of faithfully making payments on a mortgage upon which little time or money remained, they were unable to pay it off. They were forced to walk away from their life's work and the home we had all held so dear. No longer was I able to run across the fields and into my grandmother's kitchen or my grandfather's barn and see their smiling faces.

When Christmas came the following year, we sat around the table in a different dining room, but the people gathered were familiar, with a few new ones added. My grandparents, despite the severe setback, still had their family. When my Grandma smiled and handed me the dish of plum pudding with brown sugar sauce from her work-worn hands, I suddenly understood that Christmas is found in the heart and faces of those we love.

Gordon's Christmas Skates

(1936)

THE SUBJECT OF THIS STORY IS MY FATHER, GORDON DOUGLAS CAMPBELL. HE DIED IN 1997, SO I HAD TO TURN TO MY MOTHER AND HIS YOUNGEST SISTER, MARION MONTIGNY, TO DISCOVER THE DETAILS.

Sometimes the greatest Christmas gift you receive is not the gift itself, but rather the sacrifice someone has made to give it to you.

I was born in 1928 in a small isolated settlement called Nebraska in the community of Lot 16, Prince Edward Island. Early settlers, who were either too late or too poor to snag the better land, carved the settlement out of the woods. No one among the living ever knew where the name Nebraska came from. Its primary attribute was that it edged the Nebraska Creek, the sheltered inlet of Ellis River, which was rich in sea life. At its peak, there were thirteen small farms and homes in

Nebraska. Its people drew a meagre living from the heavy clay soil, the fishery, and by renting themselves out as day labourers to the more prosperous farmers in the surrounding settlements.

My father, Austin Campbell, and my mother, Winnifred O'Hearn, had nothing when they married, and they would have little more for years to come. But that never stopped them from striving to lift themselves and their children to a better place. Other than when there was a bottle in his hand, my father was the most gentle of men. When he replaced the bottle with the Bible not even a swear word passed his lips. I was the first of their five children and they named me Gordon Douglas. I do not know where the Gordon came from, but the Douglas was the English version of my grandfather's Scottish name, Dougal. Twenty months later my brother, Ira, was born. Some time later, three girls—Joyce, May, and Marion—arrived one after the other.

The Great Depression made up the majority of my childhood years and I witnessed hard times for many people I knew. My father was fortunate to have gainful employment during the oyster season with a large oyster producer and businessman. Even then, the oysters produced in the bays and estuaries of Prince Edward Island had an international reputation for satisfying the most exacting of palates. Due to the concern of thieves stealing the precious seafood from the river at nighttime, my father often worked overnight security, rowing a small dory from lease to lease.

When the weather was warm and the night sky clear, my mother would bundle up Ira and me and the three of us would join Daddy in the boat. It was a wonderful adventure to lie curled up in a blanket in the bottom of the dory and look up at the stars and the moon in the heavens above, while being rocked to sleep by the slow, gentle movement of the boat and the sound of the oars pushing through the water. My parents would talk softly, their voices carrying across the still water. The lantern, which couldn't defeat the darkness, never intruded on my sleep. To wake at dawn and see the mist rising from both the river and the land was a privilege for me.

If Daddy was not on night watch, he then used that same dory to fish oysters throughout the day, coming home at night with his shoulders tired and tight from using the oyster tongs. Often, he graded the oysters in the small wooden factory and packaged them in crates. For six days of hard work, he earned seven dollars. Cash was scarce and my parents had to stretch it as far as possible to keep the household provided with items that could not be grown, caught, found, or made.

Our family consumed a hundred pounds of flour a month, for bread was a staple. One bag of flour cost seven dollars, which was one week's pay. Molasses usually topped the bread, and there were times when there was simply no money to refill the molasses jug. I remember clearly the day my mother asked Ira and me to take the empty jug to the store and ask for it to be filled on credit. No doubt she thought the chances of it happening were better for two small boys than a grown woman. The answer at the store was no, and my hurt pride would not allow me to let neighbours see us walk back to Nebraska with an empty jug. I devised a plan. I slipped my fingers through the handle on one side and ordered Ira to do the same on the other side, and we carried that jug as though the weight of its fullness was almost too much for two young boys.

When he was not fishing oysters, Daddy fished lobsters in the inlet, speared eels, dug clams, jigged cod, or whatever else the sea gave up. At the same time, he worked a small plot of land growing potatoes, turnips, and a little hay and grain. We all worked in the garden, spring through fall, and picked whatever wild fruit we could find. Daddy raised a pig, chickens for both meat and eggs, and, if at all possible, a cow. A horse was essential for travel. He cut wood to heat our small house, which itself was a hand-me-down, and did whatever other work he could to put food on our table. Since my mother was wonderful at making a little go a long way, we were fortunate to rarely know the pangs of hunger. She sewed our clothing and knit our socks, mittens, and hats. We always looked presentable and clean, for one of her favourite sayings was, "You can be poor, but you don't have to be dirty."

I was an adventurous child and my imagination was well developed. The word "bored" was not in my vocabulary. The Great Depression had added to my parent's hardship, so Ira and I made fun, rather than expecting it to come in a package or over the airwaves. We explored the woods and built forts from scraps of wood. We walked the shoreline looking for interesting finds and we learned to swim like little seals from the side of Daddy's boat. We thought up ways to tease the two bachelor brothers who lived next door and who sometimes helped themselves to the eggs in our henhouse. Stuffing a jute bag down their chimney to smoke out their house was not beyond us.

We joined with the other children for miles around to play games like tag, kick the can, hide-and-seek, red rover, and baseball. In the winter, we waited impatiently for the creek to freeze over so we could play pond hockey. Those of us without skates played in our boots and found whatever we could for a stick. On that pond we were all heroes, and, whatever problems we may have been facing, the "real world" faded away. I dreamed of having skates: gliding over the ice with speed and skill, chasing after the puck, carrying it to the net, shooting, and scoring. The money, however, was just not there for such a luxury item so boots continued to serve as my skates.

I loved to watch my father skate in his beautiful black boot skates that he owned long before he was married. I suppose they were the only item he owned that was strictly his and served no purpose other than pleasure. I never doubted that they meant a great deal to him, which made his gesture so surprising when I reached age eight.

At the start of skating season, he announced it was time for me to learn to skate properly, but because there was no money for skates of my own, I would use his. He sat me down and he placed my feet, still wearing my winter boots, inside his beautiful black skates. As he began to lace them up he said, "They won't be a perfect fit, but they will do until you have your own."

He was right—they were not perfect. I wobbled and turned over my ankles as I struggled to gain control of both the skates and my movement on the ice, but day after day, I put them on and headed for the pond with Ira, in his boots, trailing jealously behind me. And each time, through sheer determination and practice, I got a little more skilled at skating. I soon reached a point where I could control both the skates and the hockey puck.

I must admit that I was not always respectful of my father's sacrifice. One day, as I set out for the pond, I came around the corner of the house, head down, cursing a blue streak at how awkward the skates felt on my feet. I looked up to see my father standing in front of me and stopped quickly, feeling my heart sink into the pit of my gut. I knew I had done wrong in several ways and was on the verge of losing the privilege of wearing his skates.

I stood looking at him as he stood looking at me.

After what seemed like a long time but in reality was mere moments, he said, "Young fellow, you better not let your mother hear you speak like that," and he walked away. I was very fortunate, for I think Daddy saw that even with skates that did not fit, I was becoming a skilled skater and hockey player, and he did not want to interfere with a dream.

The following winter, as Christmas drew near, our parents told us we could each ask Santa for one thing. I wanted to declare my longing for skates, but I was certain Santa was in no position to grant such a wish. I said I would leave it up to him. As usual, Christmas would consist of stockings from Santa, a special chicken dinner, and a relaxed day for the family that might include visits from neighbours and friends.

On Christmas Eve, all of us children were excited, but I more so than the others. I had a feeling that something very special was coming my way. When it came time to hang our stockings by the stove, I was struck with a strong, spontaneous idea.

"My stocking isn't big enough for what Santa is bringing," I said to Ira. "I'm going to put out my sweater." Ira looked at me as though I had suddenly grown a second set of ears.

"Are you kidding? You know Santa brings an apple, an orange, some barley candy, and one small gift that will likely be socks or pyjamas. Your stocking can hold all that."

But I could not be persuaded otherwise. I was still very much experiencing a sixth sense of something important about to happen, so I hung up the thick, bulky sweater my mother had knit for me the past fall.

We went to bed but I did not sleep very well—excitement and trepidation filled me. Questions swirled in my mind as I relived my earlier impetuous decision. Why had I hung the sweater? I wasn't trying to be greedy, but Santa wouldn't know that. What if he left nothing? If the sweater was empty in the morning, Ira would tease me for months. After what seemed like hours, I drifted into a restless sleep.

The next thing I knew Ira was pounding on me to get up. Dawn was breaking and surely Santa had come. We crept out of bed. The cold of the unheated room hit our bodies and we quickly scrambled into our clothing and forced ourselves to walk slowly to the stairs. We stopped short at the top tread for we could see lamplight coming from the kitchen and heard movement. What if Santa had only just arrived? Then we heard the cover of the stove rattle and Daddy speaking to Mom. We tore down the stairs and into the warm kitchen. We ignored the adults as our eyes went directly to the stockings and sweater.

Yes! There was something bulging in the sweater!

"Boys, I think you should wait for your sisters to get up," said Mom.

But Daddy saved the day. "It's Christmas, Winnifred. Let them go ahead—the girls could sleep for a long time yet."

It was then that I noticed Daddy seemed as excited as Ira and I. I was trembling as I raced across the kitchen to where the sweater hung on the hook behind the stove, but I tried to be patient and allowed Ira to take down his stocking first. I watched as he sat down and began to remove its contents. As he had predicted the night before, there was an apple, the only orange he would taste all year, and a handful of precious barley candy. He turned the apple and the orange over and over in his hands before picking up the brown paper parcel. He had been right about the gift as well—beautifully knit socks and mittens.

Now it was my turn. I reached for the sweater to lift it from the hook. It was heavy. Not only was there something in each sleeve, but something in the body of the sweater itself! With great anticipation, I lowered myself to the kitchen floor and slowly parted the bottom of the sweater to look inside. I could not believe my eyes. With Ira hollering for me to take out the contents, I slowly reached inside to run my hand over the smooth surface of a black skate boot. Gingerly, I lifted the pair from their hiding place and looked in awe at my very own skates.

Ira's mouth fell open in astonishment. "Why would Santa bring skates for Gordon and not me?"

Daddy carefully answered, explaining that Santa must have understood that it was time for me to have skates of my own so that Ira would be able to use his skates. He went on to say that because Ira had grown so much in the past year, he would now be able to start learning to skate the way I had. My brother beamed with pride knowing that Santa had felt he was ready for this important step.

Daddy said Santa had left a note for me and he handed it over. Mom, Daddy, and Ira listened intently as I read it aloud.

Dear Gordon,

I hope you will enjoy your skates. Since times are a little hard right now, I had to give you a pair that another boy has out-grown. But the elves did a beautiful job making them look as good as new. I selected a pair that is a little bigger than what you need right now so they will last longer. The lovely heavy wool socks your mother knits for you will make them fit just right. When Ira puts on your father's skates I expect you to help him learn to skate as well as you can. I will be watching. I will return next year.

Santa

The elves had, indeed, made the skates look like new—not that it mattered to me. I finally had a pair of skates to call my own. I barely glanced at the apple, orange, and candy in the sleeves of the sweater. I only had eyes for the skates.

We didn't even wait for the girls to get up to see what might be in their stockings. Daddy helped lace up my new skates, and then put his skates over Ira's boots and the three of us headed for the pond. Our father played net and time seemed to stand still. Had Daddy not told us we had to go back to the house, we would have skipped Christmas dinner. If I had a nickel for every hour I spent in those skates over the next several years, I would have been a rich boy.

By the time I outgrew them, I was earning my own money picking potatoes and turnips in the fall and completing whatever work I could on Saturdays with neighbouring farmers. I also had my own trapline. I was able to buy myself new skates but strangely, I was never as attached to them as I was those first skates Santa brought.

In the intervening years, I learned Daddy had saved a cent here and a cent there to earn those skates for me. My mother told me how determined he was that I would have skates of my own. And he did the same for Ira and the girls. The skates were truly special to me, but they were nothing in comparison to the tangible evidence of my father's love.

When I became a father, Santa delivered gifts to my children and my wife and I always had a present under the tree for them from us. Even though it was often a sacrifice, for money was not plentiful, I always placed my own personal gift for each of them under the tree. I wanted to see the pleasure and excitement on their faces my Daddy had seen on mine.

I believe it was a way to repay the father who taught me that love is not a word, but an action that sometimes involves sacrifice. Every year, it renewed in my heart the true meaning of Christmas.

A Christmas Goodbye

(1941)

ON A BEAUTIFUL SUNDAY AFTERNOON IN SEPTEMBER 2012, I DROPPED BY MELVIN STETSON'S HOME IN FREETOWN, PEI. MELVIN AND HIS WIFE, GRACE, WELCOMED ME. I WAS HON-OURED MELVIN SHARED A STORY SO CLOSE TO HIS HEART. (MELVIN DIED ON NOVEMBER 13, 2015.)

When I was a child, Christmas was a simple affair. It was a time for us to draw closer, share the blessings of family love, and enjoy the magic of the season. While memories of many of those childhood Christmases bring a smile to my face, there is one I recall with bitter sweetness. But before I speak of Christmas 1941, let me set the stage.

With the North American economy rapidly descending into a disastrous depression, 1930 may not have been the ideal time to expand a family. But that was the reality for my parents, Elizabeth and Fred Stetson. They farmed a small acreage in South Freetown and while the harvest of 1929 had been a bountiful one for Island farmers, PEI was not insulated from the world economy. The beautiful landscape and soothing daily rituals of farm life were no doubt the envy of many in those hard times of recession.

My parents were no strangers to hardship. Side by side, they planted and harvested the fields, tended the various livestock, and worried about the returns on their labour. In addition my mother cared for the household and, along with my father, parented their four-year-old daughter, Anna.

Now Elizabeth was pregnant again, and instinct told her it was twins. But Doctor Henry Moyse, beloved country doctor from Bedeque, assured her "it was all good" and there was just one heartbeat. Mother didn't argue with the good doctor, but she knew two babies were growing in her womb. She was not surprised when her work was interrupted on a hot day in July with the pangs of premature labour. Father went for Doctor Moyse, who was indeed surprised, and by the time the two men arrived back at the farmhouse on the Drummond Road, my twin sister, Margaret, had been born. I, ever the gentleman, was waiting my turn to greet the world. They named me Melvin.

Growing up on a farm in Freetown gave me no cause for complaint. Sheltered from the concerns of the world, I was a happy boy as our family continued to grow. Four years after the birth of Margaret and me, another girl, Freda, was added to our family, followed in another two years by a boy, Chester. We were a hardy, healthy gang of five and we lived in our own paradise. Even our father's progressive heart problems did not greatly impact us—our mother picked up his workload and hid the worry well.

Our farm sat near a gentle dip in the land that gave way to a small valley with a fast-running brook that was ideal for wading and fishing. The hills were perfect for winter sledding and summer biking, and the woodland was perfect for adventure-filled activities fed by vivid imaginations. Our farm chores were not a burden and, while not fancy, there was always food on our plates and handmade clothing on our backs.

Christmas was a simple time. The few gifts we found on Christmas morning were the work of our mother. No matter how hard the times, she made sure we each had a stocking that held at least an orange, an apple, and some barley candy.

People were often surprised that although I was a twin, it was my older sister, Anna, who was my soulmate. Make no mistake, Margaret and I loved each other and got along well, but right from the beginning we were different souls following our own paths. Anna and I connected in a way that I still do not fully understand and cannot explain.

Margaret developed an interest in baking, cooking, and needlework, all of which were such help to my work-weary mother. Anna and I shared a love of the outdoors, the farm, horses, skating, hockey, checkers, and crokinole. We rarely ever fought and she was what one imagines a big sister to be—a protector.

On the day I was to start school, I refused to go. Mother wisely said nothing and allowed me to stay home. As I watched Anna and Margaret walk down the lane to join up with the other children walking to the schoolhouse, I knew I didn't want to be left behind. The next day I was ready and waiting. Anna, who was four years ahead of me, kept watch over me that day and many more to come.

As we grew, the Great Depression gave way to the Second World War and though times grew no easier, we took comfort in family. All too soon Anna was ready to embark on a new chapter in her life. When she completed grade ten at the country school, Anna enrolled in the business course at Summerside High School. It meant my beloved sister would have to move to Summerside, some nine miles away, and be away from us all week. But I was happy for her.

That summer flew by. Mother sewed new outfits and secured a room in a boarding house in town. Anna needed ration tickets for food and, finally, a train ticket. The day she left I stood bravely at the Freetown train station and waved her on towards this new adventure.

When I began grade seven at the South Freetown School that fall, things were different. I waited with anticipation for the weekends. Anna's visits were always full of details about life in town.

But something was not right with Anna. She consistently felt unwell, and after a visit to the doctor, he found a lump on her chest. It was removed at the Prince County Hospital but came back, to the puzzlement of the doctors. Regardless of how many times they removed it, it reappeared and she grew weaker. When she came home to Freetown for the Christmas break, it was obvious she would not be able to go back to school.

My parents were very concerned. They followed the advice of the doctor and made arrangements to take Anna to Kentville, Nova Scotia, to see a specialist. Mother and Anna took Joe Davidson's ambulance from Kensington while the rest of us stayed home and carried on. How long they were gone I cannot say, but it was long enough that Mother had to work in the hospital kitchen to help pay the medical bill and her own board. Mother refused to talk about the experience other than to say she often looked out the window of the hospital and wondered which way was home.

Then the test results came back. The specialist spoke to my mother with little compassion or understanding of a mother's love for her child.

"How did you get here?" he asked.

When she told him he responded, "Then you better get the ambulance back here and go home. She might not be alive when you get there."

It was her first realization that Anna was not going to recover.

Anna survived the trip home, and we decided she would have everything she wanted in her remaining time. Her lungs began to fill with fluid and her breathing became more and more difficult. The fresh outdoor air seemed to ease her gasps, so we took turns taking her about in a hand sleigh. When she could no longer climb the stairs of the house, we made a bedroom for her downstairs.

With Father and Anna both sick, Mother's workload increased even more. I often stayed home from school to help and the carefree days of youth began to slip away. I spent whatever time I could with Anna. No matter how awful she felt, she always remained the gentle, grateful Anna I knew and loved.

Winter turned to spring, then summer, and with the arrival of autumn we were grateful Anna was still with us. Christmas was coming round again. Though no one said it, I believe we all understood we had been given the gift of one last Christmas with her. We were determined it would be no different from any other Christmas. Sickness would not be a guest of the holiday.

One afternoon my mother gave me the responsibility of taking the horse and sleigh to the village to buy groceries. It was a position of trust for a boy of twelve and I was determined to make her proud. Anna asked to accompany me, and much to our surprise, Mother and Father agreed. I hitched our driving mare, Ruby, to the jaunting sleigh and helped Anna onto the seat.

Though it was a beautiful winter afternoon, it was cold, so I wrapped the heavy buffalo robe around both of us. When I gently tapped the reins on Ruby's back, the keen little mare was off, bells on her harness ringing delightfully in the crisp air. There were no cars in sight and only sleigh tracks on the road. I felt quite important driving toward the village with Anna by my side. There was much to see and Anna's head darted about taking it all in.

The village of Freetown was picture-perfect with its neatly kept houses, train station, post office, three general stores, and potato warehouses. We took our time in the store drinking in the sights, sounds, and—best of all—the delightful smells. When our order was complete we could linger no longer and I stowed the groceries and helped Anna back up into the sleigh. I turned Ruby toward home.

But Anna was in no rush to go back to the house. She begged me to take the long way back, which would add at least three miles to our journey. Wanting to please her, I agreed, never thinking of the worry it would cause at home. We set off slowly and listened to the bells and the crisp, clear echo of Ruby's hoofs on frozen snow. We talked about things dear to our hearts.

As we passed each home on the road, Anna looked in and made a kind comment about every family as though trying to commit them to memory. I slowed Ruby to a walk for both Anna and I wanted to make that sleigh ride last forever. The moments were golden and filled with peace. And yet the joy was tinged with a sorrow that penetrates deep into the heart. All too soon we were entering back into the farm lane and pulling up to the front door, from which concerned adults hurried to both scold and laugh.

Christmas Day was a good one for all of us. Despite it being wartime and many things being rationed, there were stockings and little gifts to open and enjoy. We gratefully savoured our Christmas dinner and every seat at the table was occupied. The most thankful of us all was Anna.

Christmastime gave way to 1942, and January turned to February. On the sixth day of the month, early in the morning, Anna called out for our mother and father. She asked them to sit by her bed and hold her hands. As they did so, Anna spoke of all that she was grateful for. Then, peacefully, she was gone. Her obituary included these words: "For those who march forward with God, he healeth the broken hearts. He bindeth up their wounds."

I never really got over Anna's death. Even as a man of eighty-two, I find it hard to speak of her although I know it is healing to do so. When people ask if I still feel her presence, all I can do is smile half-heartedly and shake my head no. Tears spring into my eyes and run down my cheeks to my lips where I taste their saltiness. I wonder if Anna is present in those tears after all—for she was salt of the earth.

Laura's Worst Christmas

(1941)

I WROTE THIS STORY AFTER AN INTERVIEW WITH LAURA BELLE MILLAR PHILLIPS OF ARLINGTON. I HAD GONE FOR A VISIT AND AS WE SAT IN HER WARM COZY KITCHEN, I ASKED IF SHE REMEMBERED HER BEST CHRISTMAS EVER. HER ANSWER WAS UNEXPECTED. SHE EXPRESSED ANNOY-ANCE THAT ALL THE GOOD CHRISTMAS CELEBRATIONS SHE HAD KNOWN BLENDED TOGETHER AND IT WAS HER WORST CHRISTMAS THAT STOOD OUT.

I was born on June 14, 1928, in the community of Mount Pleasant in Prince County, Prince Edward Island. I was given the name Laura Belle. I was the tenth child in a family of fourteen, though my youngest sibling, Edgar, died at just two months of age. I was privileged to grow up in such a large family, which was common for the day.

My parents had no problem—at least that I know of—feeding such a brood. My father, Arthur Edgar Millar, had established himself before he married my mother, Florence Maud Ramsay, at the age of twenty-nine. In his early twenties he went to Boston and worked with the ice teams. He travelled the streets of that great American city that has claimed so many Islanders, delivering blocks of ice to the ice chests of home after home. He banked the majority of his wage for the future he had planned. He was never tempted to make Boston home, for waiting for him on the Island was a girl. When the time was right, he came back to PEI, married my mother, and used his savings to buy two farms in two separate districts—one in Mount Pleasant and the other in Port Hill.

It was on the Mount Pleasant farm the newlyweds settled and raised cattle and foxes. It was the heyday of the silver fox industry, which was founded on the Island and took the world by storm; it was not unusual for my father to sell a pelt for seven hundred dollars or more. It was amazing money for the day and once the Great Depression descended, the industry helped buffer many an Island farmer.

In October 1929, when I was just over the age of one, my parents bought and moved to a farm in Birch Hill. My mother felt that, with ten children, they needed a bigger house. The property owner, David Dougherty, was more than eager to sell to my parents because a family with that many children would certainly assist in keeping the nearby Presbyterian Church afloat for years to come.

The move proved to be a wise one—even more children arrived to fill the rooms of the stately two-storey home, which not only had a kitchen range but a wood and coal floor furnace that radiated heat throughout the house. The cattle and the crops thrived on the fertile land of Birch Hill, as did the foxes in the quiet setting of the big fox ranch.

We children also thrived. We were close to both the school and the church and we blended well into the community. We made friends easily, many of whom we often brought home after school. We raided the fox biscuit barrels for a good snack and I sometimes wonder if that is why we had such a fine sheen to our hair and skin.

There were many surprises in my young life, one of which was the boxes of clothing my Aunt Pearl sent or brought to PEI from the United States, where she privately taught two sons of a wealthy family. Her boxes were so varied they even contained evening dresses, which we always fawned over. We loved to imagine the parties that the ladies had attended. Many of the dresses fit my older sisters perfectly, and our mother would use her sewing skills to make the rest of us new dresses, skirts, blouses, and jumpers from the cut-down material of the ones that didn't fit anyone. Pants were not a fashion item I had the opportunity to wear until I got a hand-me-down pair from Gladys Hayes. They were too short but I hardly cared—I was the only one in school to have a pair and they made me stand out from the crowd. Mom was not a knitter so she would take her wool to a lady with a knitting machine to have our socks, hats, and mittens made. We were always well turned out.

Christmas was a time of anticipation and pure joy in my childhood home. There was a school concert and a church concert to prepare for and starting early in December we would busy ourselves with memorizing our parts until they could be said with ease and grace. Santa Claus, whose mannerism reminded me somehow of my father, always showed up at the school concert and each child would receive a small gift from the teacher.

It was the tradition of the time to not begin Christmas preparations until just before the big day. I believe it made the excitement even more intense. Mom and Dad would go to Summerside, the capital of Prince County, on the train just a few days prior to Christmas. Though we children knew they were cutting it close to the big day we never worried, for we were confident in their adult wisdom. While in Summerside, Dad bought raisins and grapes: a rare and special treat. Our mouths would water with anticipation as we waited for him to get home because they did not have to be saved for Christmas day.

On Christmas Eve day my older brothers, Don and George, would go to the woods at the back of the farm to find a Christmas tree. It was a great adventure for them and they took their time selecting a fine fir to grace our parlour. It was a matter of pride for the boys to make a selection that would awe the rest of the family. My mother would decorate it with red rope and coloured balls in the evening after everyone else had gone to bed so it would be a surprise for us on Christmas morning.

I never asked Santa for a particular gift; I understood the choice was up to him. It was always difficult to sleep on Christmas Eve. I would toss and turn wondering what Santa would bring, while at the same time being consumed with worry that I might not be asleep before he arrived (Santa always left our wool stockings filled with treats by our beds). Apparently, this was to allow our mother some freedom on Christmas morning to prepare the two geese without all of us underfoot.

The moment our eyes opened on the morning of Christmas and fell upon the stockings, we sprang into action and tore into them. For certain, there would be an orange, barley candy, and homemade fudge. Sometimes the girls would get homemade dolls with round, cotton cloth heads, embroidery eyes, yarn hair, and a stuffed body. Often the gift in the sock was clothing, either store-bought or handmade. One year my brothers Don and George found cap guns in their stockings. They shot off every last cap before they even got out of bed, and their fun was quickly over.

There was no gift exchange in our home, other than the stockings, until my older siblings joined the workforce and began to bring home store-bought presents at Christmastime. How I loved *Heidi*, the book my brother Erland gave me one year, and the actual doll Helen brought from Sharpe's Store in Tyne Valley where she worked as a clerk. We spent Christmas Day enjoying our gifts, Christmas dinner, and family. For me, no other time of year could match the simple wonder of Christmas. It was a day of magic, and I believed it would always be that way.

But disillusion was to come in my thirteenth year.

Our home had an unwelcome and feared visitor arrive in the days before Christmas: red measles. One by one, my siblings—Don, George, Priscilla, and Ruth—came down with the contagious virus. It started with a fever, runny nose, hacking cough, and red eyes, and progressed to a reddish, blotchy rash. They were confined to their beds in darkened rooms, and no one was allowed near them other than Mom and Dad. The feeling of strain replaced the feeling of Christmas. Though no one ever said it aloud, we all knew measles could result in pneumonia or brain swelling, which could then lead to permanent brain damage, hearing loss, or even death.

Good nursing was the only defence, and Mom embraced the task to the point that she had no time to think of Christmas preparations. Don and George were Dad's helpers in the barn so my younger sister Rowena and I were named their replacements. We found ourselves working hard outdoors rather than relaxing and preparing for Christmas. But even more worrisome than the work was the fact that Don and George always made the trek to the woods for the Christmas tree. It was not looking good for the Millar family Christmas of 1941.

Christmas Eve day dawned clear and cool, but it was unlike any other Christmas Eve day I had ever known. Rowena and I spent the day in the barnyard cutting wood with a crosscut saw. My father mixed green wood with the dry wood stacked in the woodhouse to make it go further in the kitchen range and furnace. We were not overly swift at the job for it takes real coordination to move the saw smoothly back and forth without jamming it. It took hours of sawing and worked every muscle in our bodies.

As daylight began to fade, we joined our father in the barn for evening chores. My job was to hold the lantern while he fed the livestock. One would not dare set the lantern down among the hay or straw in fear of starting a fire. Usually I enjoyed the job and would stand silently in the warm barn listening to the quiet stirring of the cattle and horses as they consumed their evening meal and settled themselves in the darkness. But on this occasion, all I could think of was the lack of Christmas preparations and how I could rectify it. I spoke softly to Rowena.

With the chores completed, the three of us left the barn and walked out into the dark. Rowena and I put our plan to our father.

"Dad, we need a tree or it will not be Christmas," I said.

He stood quietly and with the light of the lantern, looked at our expectant faces. He agreed that a tree was indeed part of the holiday. He paused, looked into the darkness, and then back to our faces.

"Get the saw and axe," he said.

With only the light of the lantern to guide us, Dad, Rowena, and I began the walk to the swamp—a short distance behind the barn.

We felt no fear in the dark thanks to our father. We stopped at the first tree we came upon. It was not a fir, but rather a spruce and was not very tall or handsome. It was an evergreen, though, so we cut it down. Rowena and I hauled it home behind our father who lit the way with the lantern. We found a board to nail the tree to and stood it up in our parlour. Usually the Christmas tree the boys brought home stopped just beneath the eleven-foot ceiling. Our spruce tree barely reached the top of the door frame...but we had a tree. The children who were not sick helped Mom decorate and as each ornament was placed, the spirit of Christmas grew. The house was filling with belief that the children in their beds would recover.

It seems Santa did not fear the measles, for all of us children found filled stockings on our beds come morning. Strangely, I do not even remember what I received. This was the first Christmas I could not spend in bed enjoying my gift—I had to go to the barn, do up the chores, and saw yet more wood. My mother served her usual delicious Christmas dinner and we all savoured it, even though we were missing our sister Fern and her husband Nelson; Fern was expecting her first baby and couldn't risk catching the measles.

But in the afternoon, we heard a sound in the yard. Fern had never been away from home for Christmas and even if it was just for a moment, she needed to be there. All of the children were herded upstairs and she and Nelson came into the kitchen and looked in the parlour to see our ugly tree. She left wrapped gifts for all of us children on the table and was on her way. We waved to her and Nelson through the bedroom windows.

Come evening, it was back to the barn for Rowena and me. It was the busiest Christmas I had known in my young life. Thankfully, all my siblings fully recovered, but all these years later I still think of that Christmas as the "worst."

Yet the wisdom of age brings clarity and even if it was not a perfect holiday, it was full of family and love—the true spirit of the season could not be defeated. Even during my "worst" Christmas, the light of the season shone through. It is Christmas 1941 I remember when so many of the perfect ones have faded.

A Test of
Christmas Faith

(1942)

CLAUDIA CAMERON KEMBER GREW UP ON CAMERON'S
HILL IN SOUTHWEST, LOT 16. THOUGH SHE NOW CALLS
DARTMOUTH, NOVA SCOTIA, HOME, SHE COMES BACK OFTEN
TO VISIT HER CHILDHOOD COMMUNITY. A CONVERSATION
WITH CLAUDIA IN MY MOTHER'S KITCHEN ON A BEAUTIFUL
FALL DAY IN 2013 WAS THE GENESIS OF THIS STORY.

Even before my eyes were open, I knew the bedroom was
brighter than usual. It could only mean one thing. Ignoring
the cold, I jumped from my bed and ran to the window. Yes! The
first snow of the season had fallen overnight. The ground was
covered with a light dusting that transformed the farmyard and
steep hill running down to the river into a glittering white carpet
sparkling in the morning sun. From my second-storey window in
the farmhouse, I had the perfect view of this new world. I appreciated the scene in the manner of a child—with pure delight.

The water in the Southwest River inlet that led to Nebraska Creek was frozen, though I knew there would not yet be any depth to the ice. This meant no more rum-running schooners sailing into the inlet where the crews threw wooden kegs into the marsh. Many a night I would watch from my bedroom window on Cameron Hill for the lantern light of the local bootlegger stealthily moving down the hill to collect his deliveries.

My father would not allow my brother, Lloyd, or me around the river for most of the year because of the RCMP officers who lay in wait for the bootlegger or sailboats. With the onset of winter, though, Lloyd and I would soon be able to skate on the river and explore the marshes and woodland with no fear of unexpected encounters or danger.

But the snow and cold held an even deeper meaning—concrete evidence that Christmas was on the way. I was certain I could smell it in the frosty air that penetrated the walls of my unheated bedroom. I rushed to dress and hurried downstairs for breakfast. This was one time I could not wait to be off to school. My cousins would be waiting for me at the end of their lane and we could talk about how the snow would make it easier to find the tracks of Santa's sleigh and reindeer—he would be checking in to see if we were good or bad in the days leading up to Christmas.

The walk to and from school and the time in the classroom was my only opportunity to visit my cousins. Though I longed to go to their home I was not welcome, nor were they welcome at my house—all because of an old grudge between my uncle and my father.

My father had not planned to farm on Cameron Hill in the community of Lot 16. As a young man he went west to Moose Jaw, Saskatchewan, to work on a grain farm. He easily adapted to life in the west and had no plans of coming home. His father wanted him to return to PEI and accept his heritage as the youngest male, which meant taking over the family farm. It had long been in the Cameron name; decades previously it had been carved from forests filled with Native summer camps which the British had claimed as Crown land. The original grantee had been Alexander Cameron, who had sailed his schooner from the Isle of Skye, Scotland, to the shores of Prince Edward Island. Alexander's seven sons had spread out through Lot 16, Wellington, and Richmond, passing their lands down through generations.

When Grandfather Cameron fell ill, my father finally came home to Cameron Hill to take up his legacy. That very action was to have long-term consequences. His older brother, Russell, "set up" by his father on the farm next door, had hoped to eventually own both farms. When my father came back, Russell's hopes were dashed and the rift between them never mended, even though they lived side by side and could have been such a help and comfort to each other.

My cousins, brother, and I never allowed our parents' quarrel to affect us and we had such fun together. The day of the first snow would be no different. We could finally begin planning what we wanted Santa to fill our stockings with. In my short lifespan, Christmas had always been good. The festival held a special place in the hearts of my parents and we looked forward to celebrating the season together each year.

I was the second and final child of William and Margaret Cameron, born on August 13, 1937. They named me Claudia Adrice. It was a spur-of-the-moment decision, for my parents had chosen the name Edith Gloria prior to my birth. However, after Dr. Claude Simpson and his nurse Adryce Campbell safely delivered me, my name was changed to honour them both, although they chose a different spelling. I was royally welcomed and treated as a special little girl.

My brother, Lloyd John Joseph, was six when I was born. My parents treated him very generously as well, for they were grateful he was alive. At age five, Lloyd developed spinal meningitis: an inflammation of the protective membranes covering the brain and spinal cord. He survived the outbreak of the disease, which claimed over twenty children in the surrounding areas of Cameron Hill in 1936. It left his spine like jelly and claimed most of his hearing and his speech. For two long years, the only way he could turn in bed was if someone wrapped him in a sheet to protect his spine while they flipped him over. Lloyd was seven before he could walk again and he stuttered for many years as he regained his speech. His hearing never fully returned.

My parents were firm believers in Santa Claus and were impressed with how he indulged their children. One year he brought me a plastic frog and Lloyd a train. Another year, I got a wooden rocker. Our homemade, itchy woollen socks were always full on Christmas morning with surprises like oranges, barley candy, fudge, clothing, and small toys.

There was no reason to think this Christmas, my sixth, would be any different. With the arrival of the snow and

December slipping by on the calendar, Lloyd and I made our lists for Santa, but something strange was afoot. Excited as we were for the coming holiday, we could see the worry on the faces of Mom and Dad. And then, just like that, they lost their faith in Santa Claus.

The week before Christmas, they sat us down in the parlour just before bedtime and broke the news: Santa was not coming this year. Of course, we would still have Christmas—we would decorate the house and eat Christmas dinner—there would just be no visit from Santa. We stared at them in total surprise.

"But why? What's wrong with Santa?" I asked.

Mom and Dad sat silently for a moment and then, with a nod from Mom, Dad began to explain. For some unknown reason, our potato harvest had broken down and rotted in storage. All the work, investment, and income from the crop was gone. The Christmas money, earned from fishing oysters and the sale of the fall pig, would have to be used to pay bills.

Lloyd and I were totally confused. What did any of this have to do with Santa? Surely the failed crop had nothing to do with him. We did not question our parents further—it was obvious they were worried about many things and maybe that was why they had lost faith in Santa. Lloyd and I were not about to give up on him. Maybe he would not bring as much this year, but surely he would bring something, for we had been good.

Several days before Christmas, Mom and Dad began decorating the house. Dad went to the woods at the back of the farm and brought home a fir tree, which he stood in the family parlour. Here, we would enjoy the tree until Old Christmas (or Epiphany) on January 6; a day to remember the three wise men's visit to baby Jesus. I helped Mom decorate the tree with cardboard stars wrapped in the shiny foil from the Salada tea package. When light caught the silver, the tree was a masterpiece. The only other decoration in the parlour was a green and red rope of twisted crêpe paper strung across the room.

Dad made a white birch centrepiece for the table. He split a short log in half and sanded down the bottom so it lay flat. In the centre of the rounded top, he drilled three holes and placed in three taper candles. Mom made fudge which, along with some peanuts in the shell, graced the table alongside the centrepiece. We were going to my grandparents' home for Christmas dinner, so none of our geese had to be sacrificed.

The only thing different from any other year was the lack of the annual Christmas shopping trip. In previous years we would travel by horse and sleigh to Tyne Valley. Once inside the general store, Dad would press some money into our outstretched hands, and Lloyd and I would be allowed to select one small gift for each member of the family.

Christmas Eve arrived and in defiance, Lloyd and I hung our woollen socks by the stove in the parlour. Our parents may have lost faith in Santa Claus, but we certainly had not. It was all about believing.

That was the longest night of the year—neither Lloyd nor I would dare get up before dawn in case we encountered Santa. Though we woke in the darkness, we stayed put until the sky lightened. Then, with bated breath, we crept out of bed and ran to the window at the back of the house. And just like every other Christmas, we spotted the tracks of Santa's jaunting sleigh, which had circled the back of our house. We cried out with relief and excitement and headed for the parlour. Santa had indeed come, for each of our red socks held a beautiful red apple and a plump orange. We could not suppress our happiness.

When they saw the joy on our faces, Mom and Dad's faith in Santa was restored. Christmas had once again come to Cameron Hill.

Olga Returns Home for Christmas

(1942)

OLGA GAMBLE HAS BEEN A RESIDENT OF BELMONT, PEI,
FOR MOST OF HER LIFE. SHE RECOUNTED THIS STORY FOR ME
IN MARCH 2015 WHEN I WENT TO VISIT HER AT HER HOME
OVERLOOKING THE MALPEQUE BAY.

I suppose I would describe my childhood as a quiet one, but don't mistake quiet for mundane. I was born in July 1927, the daughter of Arnett Simpson and Mabel Carruthers Simpson of Belmont, PEI. They named me Olga and I suppose I would be one of the first children in our community to be born in a hospital. I still have the bill for the delivery and hospital stay, which cost $38.70.

My father, a young farmer, had met my mother when she came to the community to teach. She accepted his proposal, which included moving into the large farmhouse with his parents. My mother and her mother-in-law did well in getting along, even though there is truth to the saying "no kitchen is big enough for two women." I was the first child for my parents, and my sister, Shirley, completed our family three years later.

I was a precocious child, in part because I was raised in a household of four adults. As soon as I was capable, I was out on the farm with my father and grandfather, and as I grew, was quickly assigned one chore after another. It was my favourite place to be, for I felt connected to the earth and the animals. Indoors, I had the company of my mother, grandmother, dolls, toys, and later, Shirley. My grandmother taught me to knit, and at age four I taught myself to play the organ. I practiced so often that my father, seeing I was indeed serious, taught me to use my left hand as well. One summer, he even hired a travelling music teacher to improve my skills.

Books were a big part of my world. While my mother ironed, she practiced reading with me, so I started school already knowing how to read. My father was an amateur photographer with a small box camera and in the evenings, I was allowed to join him in the closed-off pantry to help develop his prints. He marked every picture with the date and identity of the people in the shot and filled album after album with memories.

On the afternoon of August 27, 1932, when I was five, I was contentedly sitting in our living room looking at one of the photo albums when my grandfather tore through the front door yelling, "The house is on fire—get outside!"

He and my father had been working in the yard when they noticed smoke coming out from around the bathroom pipe in the roof. My mother had the wood range going with a cake in the oven, and sparks had somehow penetrated the wall of the flue and caught something afire in the attic.

My mother grabbed my baby sister, Shirley, who was down for a nap in an upstairs bedroom, and hustled us outside. My grandmother later revealed that she had dreamed of rags for hooking mats being placed next to the flue in the attic. Upon waking, though, she forgot the dream and did not go up to check.

It didn't take long for neighbours to arrive by foot, horse, and car. The fire was burning very slowly from the top down, so people were running back and forth into the house, hauling out all our worldly goods. They were able to save doors and even the hot kitchen stove with the cake still in the oven (although a little while later we found Budd Birch's dog enjoying the cake in the field). Most important of all, we saved the photo albums.

The adults decided that Shirley and I, along with six-year-old Ralph Simmons, should be driven halfway down our long lane, out of harm's way. As the car was driving away I yelled out of the window, "Save my dolls and crayons!"

Someone summoned the fire engine from Summerside, but when it arrived, it could not access water from the hand pump. By the following morning, all that remained of our Queen Anne–style house was the foundation. Fortunately, most of our furniture had been rescued and a house on the Fraser farm just down the road sat empty.

The loss greatly affected Christmas 1932. Our tree decorations had been stored in the attic and burned in the fire. In the grand scheme of things, their loss seemed inconsequential but the tree was an important part of our family celebration. Dad always took a photo of the decorated tree, labelled it, and pasted it in the current album. That year, with a new house having to be built for our family in the midst of the Great Depression, there was no money to spare for non-essentials such as tree decorations.

Considering the circumstances, my parents could have forgone a tree that Christmas, but they understood the value of continuity and wanted to make the holiday as normal as possible. They erected a Christmas tree in our temporary home but left it bare of all human decoration. Dad took a picture, labelled it, and pasted it into the photo album. It served as a reminder that all things can be overcome.

Ten years later in 1942, I would need to remember that lesson.

A few months after the fire, we erected a new house on the burnt-out foundation of the old one. Bit by bit, the elegant interior came together.

I started school and advanced quickly. Since I could already read, I completed grades one and two in the first year and grades three and four in the second year. I soon discovered a passion for numbers and I loved to figure out equations in my head; my teacher could not give me enough double addition sums to complete.

The years passed swiftly and I completed grade ten twice because in the Belmont School, it was the highest level I could attain. I was fifteen and the Second World War had replaced the Great Depression. My parents held a discussion on the matter of my future. It was clear that I must have a way to earn a living and would have to take up one of the two occupations available for intellectual women: teaching or nursing. Since my mother and two of her sisters had been teachers, my mother and father chose teaching. It never crossed anyone's mind that I might take over the farm.

I did not argue their decision, but it meant leaving home—something I had never done other than to briefly vacation with my cousins or maternal grandparents. I would have to go to Prince of Wales College in Charlottetown, some fifty miles away, to acquire grades eleven and twelve and then my teaching license. I had been to the capital city three times in my life—twice to the Provincial Exhibition and once to see the King and Queen of England—and always with the security of family.

Fortunately, three of my cousins from Augustine Cove were also attending the college and we were to live together. We chose the third floor of a boarding house directly across the street from the college, and along with the bedrooms, we had a small bathroom and kitchen. We could make our own breakfast, but would eat the other two meals in the dining room with the rest of the boarders. My parents packed up their old car and drove me to Charlottetown. It is hard to describe the loneliness of being left there; even the company of my cousins could not take that away.

Urban life was foreign to me and I missed the routine of the farm, the house, and especially my family. I took no interest in Charlottetown, nor in the extra-curricular activities of the school. I understood giving up was not an option, so I dug in and took on both grades eleven and twelve. I did not intend to waste time, and tackled the fall term with sheer determination. I concealed, as best I could, my intense homesickness and longing for letters from home, which were rare.

When Christmas break finally arrived, I boarded the westbound train with great anticipation. I watched the landscape pass as the train took me closer and closer to my family and home. When the train reached the Miscouche Station, my father was waiting to collect me. I would have willingly walked the four miles home to Belmont, but knowing that my father had come for me was as good as an early Christmas gift.

We spent the drive sharing news after several long months of separation. When, at last, I saw the farm come into sight a wonderful feeling of contentment came over me and, once again, all was right in my world. Father put away the horse and sleigh while I ran into the house to greet the rest of the family. The sights and aromas of home filled my senses. To once again sit at the supper table and be served my mother and grandmother's cooking was immensely gratifying.

Now that I was home, I felt I could not waste a moment, but at the same time, I felt no sense of urgency. With each new dawn, I was in the barn milking cows, feeding chickens, collecting eggs, and cleaning stables. I drew pleasure from the chores and happily took on household tasks and helped Mother with her Christmas baking. In addition, I had time in the afternoons and evenings for visiting friends and family in the community.

I couldn't wait to see our neighbours—Campsie, Phyllis, Bud, Alice, and Wendell—and I believe they were equally happy to see me. We had so much to catch up on. The girls filled me in on who was dating whom, how school was going, and whatever other gossip they could think of. I may have missed out on the school Christmas concert, but I was determined that nothing else escape me. I worked hard to keep my mind in the present and pushed aside all thoughts of school and Charlottetown.

On Christmas Eve morning, my sister, Shirley, and I headed to the woods to select and cut a Christmas tree. Mother came with us to take the picture for our album. It was fun having the three of us set out on the adventure of such an important task. We searched for a well-formed tree with equally spaced limbs, but nature is not often worried about perfect design; we settled for a little less than perfection.

We brought the tree home and set it up in the dining room. In no time at all, the heat from the cast-iron radiators carried the smell of the evergreen throughout the room. Shirley and I brought down the decorations and took our time decorating the tree. When we were finished, we stood back and admired the result, already anticipating the excitement of the next day.

That evening, we prepared the food for Christmas dinner. The task did not seem daunting, for everyone worked together and we took pleasure in one another's company. Mother prepared her biggest chicken and the farm-grown vegetables. We made the stuffing and organized all the trimmings. We helped Mother with a lovely big plum pudding for dessert. Since Shirley and I were past the age of expecting Santa, we did not worry about getting to bed early.

Christmas morning started much like any other morning on a farm: the animals were waiting in the barn, so I went out with my father and grandfather to do chores while preparations for dinner continued in the house. My mother preferred to have the meal mid-afternoon, so there was no great rush to get food on the table or complete the outdoor work.

Grandfather's brother, Elijah, known to us as "Lijah," arrived for dinner with his wife, Annie, and the conversation flowed around the table. Mother and Grandmother knew how to set a beautiful table. It was covered with the hand-embroidered tablecloth upon which they placed their best dishes, silverware, and glassware. We passed around bowls of steaming vegetables, dressing, and platters of meat, piling our plates high before adding the rich gravy. We ate until we could eat no more and sighed with a mixture of contentment and agony. I realized good food and company lays the foundation for a wonderful Christmas.

When the evening came, we opened our gifts. As Shirley and I had grown older, Mother moved the unwrapping of presents to the evening to make the day last as long as possible. As always, the gifts were practical—mainly clothing. But then, Shirley handed me the envelope that had arrived a few weeks earlier from Vancouver. When I tore open the envelope and pulled out the card, a cheque for (the amazing sum of) two dollars fell out. The card was signed "Lorraine Arnett," a woman I had never met. She was my Grandmother Simpson's niece, and the only reason I could think of for her generosity was a long-held sense of gratitude to my grandmother for raising her father, Clibborn, Grandmother's younger brother, following his mother's death. Clib had gone west to British Columbia and built himself a successful construction company.

The mere sight of a two-dollar cheque was rare, and holding one was even rarer. And it was all mine! What a gift. I had a number of uses for the money, but I planned to take my time spending it so I could enjoy the sheer pleasure of having it.

I had no complaints, as Christmas drew to a close, other than to wish that both it and my childhood could last a little longer. But at least we had taken the pictures, and through them I would be able to relive the moment.

Try as I might, I could not slow time. Much too soon, it was time to return to Charlottetown and school. I told my parents I did not wish to go back, but they stood firm: I was no longer a child that could cling to home. Though I managed not to cry, the loneliness of separation gathered in me. Perhaps if I could have expressed my feelings through tears it would have been easier, but my strong memories of Christmas kept me outwardly strong.

On the morning of my departure, I was surprised to find that both my father and mother were taking me to the train. It was a silent trip, as I tried to drink in my surroundings. When we arrived at the train station, Father carried my suitcase to the passenger car. All three of us boarded, and Father stowed my case while I seated myself in a window seat. Imagine my surprise when my mother sat down beside me, and my father tipped his hat in farewell before leaving the train.

I looked at my mother in surprise. She smiled and, with a twinkle in her eye, said, "I am going to accompany you as far as Emerald—just to make sure you stay on the train." Emerald was the almost-halfway mark to Charlottetown, and the juncture where trains met to travel all four directions of the Island. My spirits lifted immediately; my mother had understood and appreciated my feelings. By choosing action over words, she showed me that I was not alone and I had a family to support me.

Mother and I enjoyed each other's company all the way to Emerald. When we parted, I was ready to continue alone knowing my cousins would be in Charlottetown to greet me. With the spirit of Christmas clinging to me, I resumed my studies and by early summer, I had completed grades eleven and twelve.

After a summer at home, I returned to the Prince of Wales College in the fall for my teacher training, secure in the knowledge I would be returning to Belmont for another family Christmas. I had strong roots and could now embrace my wings.

In the spring of 1944, I graduated fourth in a class of fifty. I was a tad annoyed and berated myself for not trying harder. Nonetheless, I was ready to face the working world as a qualified teacher. The fifteen-year-old girl who had left home two short years before was now a self-assured young woman.

Over the next ten years I taught in a number of schoolhouses and I applied myself to making school—and Christmas in particular—memorable for each student. My parents continued to welcome me home for the holidays.

At twenty-seven I married Harley Gamble, a man from my home community. Our two families joined together each Christmas and we took photos, dated them, and pasted them in the album. When I take out the many photo albums created over the years, I appreciate that there truly is no place like home for Christmas.

Grandma Maggie

(1943)

EDNA CAMERON SHEEN SHARED THE DETAILS OF THIS STORY
WITH ME IN THE FALL OF 2014 WHEN WE VISITED THE GRAVE-
SITE OF HER GRANDPARENTS.

My eyes flew open and I sat straight up in bed. I could feel my heart pounding in my chest—not with fear, but excitement. I tried to focus. What had brought me out of a deep sleep in the feather tick and warm quilts? Why was I sitting straight up in bed with the chilly air of the unheated bedroom quickly cooling my body? In a flash, I remembered: it was Christmas morning!

I instinctively knew it was early morning even though the darkness of night was still upon the house. I estimated it was somewhere between four and five, and no ordinary day would have found me awake at such an hour. I heard no sounds in the house other than a gentle snore coming from my grandparents' bedroom. I fidgeted. I knew the proper thing would be to bury myself in the warmth of the bed until I heard either Uncle Ray or Granddad go downstairs to turn up the furnace thermostat and start the fire in the kitchen range. But it was Christmas morning and my patience had run out. I had been waiting for days, on my best behaviour, for this very morning.

Quietly, I slipped from the bed and tiptoed gently to my grandparents' bedroom door. With consideration for my Aunt Edith, asleep in her bedroom, and my Aunt Dorothy and Uncle Ray asleep in their room with their toddler son, Lowell, I knocked gently on the door and in a high whisper I broke the morning silence.

"Grandma, can I get my stocking now?"

She responded, "Sure dear, go ahead."

I felt my way through the darkness to the staircase and, holding the rail, sped down the stairs and into the parlour. Our wild fir tree stood regally in one corner. I lit the oil lamp and welcomed the soft glow it gave the room, which was toasty warm from the heat of the furnace. I turned expectantly to view the tree. My stocking, handmade by my grandmother, lay beneath it, bulging with hidden treasures. I sat myself down in front of the tree and reached for the stocking.

Suddenly, my impatience was replaced by patience. Christmas came but once a year and I wanted to savour the moment and make it last as long as possible. Reaching in, I felt the roundness of the orange and after I withdrew it, I studied its perfection in both colour and shape. Oranges were a luxury throughout my life, but the rationing that accompanied the third year of the Second World War made them extra difficult to obtain. Santa's power to bypass rationing books made me respect him all the more. The barley candy came next, followed by Mrs. Santa's fudge (which seemed a lot like Grandma's). I removed the brown paper wrapping from the red mittens, and found a scarf and hat to match.

By now I was down to the bottom of the stocking and was slipping my hand in for the final parcel when Granddaddy's voice cut the silence.

"Edna, get your Aunt Edith! Maggie needs her; she isn't well."

The tone of his voice told me not to linger on that last gift. I ran to my aunt's bedroom and roused her from sleep. As a nursing supervisor in the county hospital, Aunt Edith was used to quickly springing into action and rushed to her mother's side. Aunt Dorothy quickly followed, and then my grandmother's bedroom was shut tight, leaving me in the hallway.

I stood waiting, hoping we would quickly be back to the celebration of Christmas. All of my aunts and their families would be coming later in the morning to help prepare Christmas dinner. Aunt Jessie was bringing the goose, which she was cooking at her home. The cousins would be eager to compare their Christmas gifts, admire the tree, and play games while waiting for the feast. In my thirteen years it had always been this way.

After what seemed like a long time, Aunt Dorothy emerged from the bedroom, and would only say that her mother had "taken a turn." She needed to phone my aunts and suggested I go outside to play. In that moment, I knew it was serious. It was still dark outside and most unusual for Aunt Dorothy to suggest I go out. In any case, I followed her instructions and set about putting on my outdoor clothing over my pyjamas.

The first thing I noticed when I stepped out into the cold, crisp December air was the sky: it was filled with stars shining brilliantly down on the white landscape. I grabbed my sled and began to climb the small hill behind the house. I walked up and slid down time and time again. All the while, I watched the light in my grandparents' bedroom and the shadows that passed back and forth in front of the window. Finally, I stretched out on my back and looked up at the stars. I wondered if Grandmother Maggie was now up among them, but I prayed it wasn't so, for she was my earthly angel.

I had been born out of wedlock in an age when it was considered the mother's sin but not the father's. My mother's parents, having raised a large family of their own, simply embraced me as their foster child and showed me the meaning of love. The family sheltered me as best they could from the barbs of the world.

My grandmother, an even-tempered woman, was not one to show physical affection, yet she always managed to make me feel special. Even as a young child, I felt strongly connected to her. Grandmother Maggie was of medium build with strong hands that never seemed to be still. She dressed neatly and always appreciated the clothing her sisters working in Boston sent her. It seemed she treated me as both child and equal.

I had so many wonderful memories of my grandmother. When a thunderstorm raged, Grandma, no matter my size, would carry me down the stairs and let me curl up in her lap on the rocking chair where she would soothe me with a story. She would read to me, and if I got a chill and started to shake from eating homemade ice cream too fast, she would put me in a basin of warm water with mustard powder until I was warm again. When I went to school she made sure I finished my homework, and when I came indoors on cold winter days, she ensured I stripped down and stood over the furnace to warm up. A snack would be waiting on the table.

She taught me to hook rugs, knit, sew, cook, and bake. Together we would bake bread, cookies, and cakes (my favourite being maple chocolate). She never once indicated I might be more hindrance than help. I helped her churn butter, in summer, we picked wild strawberries and raspberries, and apples in the fall. She knit my mittens and hats and made my clothing. In the rare occurrence of a spat between Grandma Maggie and Granddaddy John, I always took her part, much to his surprise.

I loved Grandma Maggie deeply. As I lay there on my back looking up at the stars, I began to think I had never told her so and it upset me profoundly. Alone and lonely, I watched the stars and darkness give way to the morning light.

Finally, I heard the sound of sleighs announcing the arrival of aunts and uncles, but no cousins, and no greetings of Christmas cheer. I followed them into the house and waited, hoping they would tell me what had happened. But precious little information came my way; whether they were attempting not to worry me, or believed children did not warrant explanation, I do not know. What I could garner was that "the turn" was either a stroke or heart attack and although Grandma Maggie was not well, she was still alive. Hope filled my heart.

The adults decided I would go with my Aunt Jessie and

Uncle Gordon to make one less chore for those who would be nursing Grandma Maggie. I was not permitted to go into her bedroom to say goodbye before I left, though I longed to see her and whisper my love. There would be no Christmas dinner for the year of 1943. I packed my suitcase and stocking, and reflected on how such a joyful day quickly became consumed with a sadness that the spirit of the season could not penetrate.

Aunt Jessie cooked the goose for Boxing Day instead, but the meal was not a joyous occasion. Life at my aunt's with my cousins was comfortable and welcoming, but I missed Grandma Maggie just as a child misses a deeply loved parent. I went through the motions of daily life and returned to school at the end of Christmas break. Grandma, lovingly cared for by her daughters, clung to life.

She marked her seventieth birthday on January 11, 1944, and received her first old-age pension cheque of three dollars. She died on January 26.

Her wake was my first trip back to the house. Granddaddy was sitting at the kitchen table when I arrived. With tears in his eyes he looked at me and said, "You will miss her terrible." No truer words have ever been spoken. I could not believe she was truly gone and I would never again hear her voice or feel her touch. I kept going back into the parlour to look at her body in the plain pine casket. My grief was overwhelming, and I could not be comforted.

The certain thing about death is that life goes on for those left behind. Christmas after Christmas came for me. I lived with my aunt and uncle, and as my mother and stepfather, living in

Halifax, Nova Scotia, began to prosper, my Christmas stocking was always full. Each year, when I reached for it beneath the tree, I would hear my Christmas angel, Grandma Maggie, gently saying, "Sure dear, go ahead."

I have never doubted the presence of angels on earth or heaven and in all the years that have come and gone, I have never forgotten or stopped missing Grandma Maggie: my angel.

A Surprise Visit to Town

(1945)

JUNE HUTCHINSON MACLEAN, WHO GREW UP IN CENTRAL, LOT 16, KINDLY SHARED THIS TREASURED STORY WITH ME. JUNE, A STORYTELLER IN HER OWN RIGHT, WAS EXCITED TO CONTRIBUTE THIS SPECIAL CHRISTMAS MEMORY TO THE COLLECTION.

My mother had a twinkle in her eye when she announced at the breakfast table one December morning that she had a surprise for me; however, I would have to wait until after the morning chores were done. I instantly dropped my fork and forgot all about the crisp farm bacon and soppy egg yolk on my plate, which I had been soaking up with a thick slab of toast made from homemade bread.

"A surprise for me? What is it? What is it?"

"Time will tell, June. Patience is a virtue, especially for five-year-old girls. All I will tell you is that this surprise is worth waiting for, so be quick about your chores."

Christmas was coming and you never knew what might be in the air. Not that I had lacked from surprises in my young life; I lived on a farm and one never knew when there might be a new calf in the barn, a baby foal in the field, or a litter of kittens in the loose hay. But somehow Christmas surprises were different.

I ran to grab my barn coat off its hook. Slipping my feet into black rubber boots, I didn't even bother to button my coat before heading out into the crisp December air. I yelled goodbye to my older brother, Bob, who was walking down the lane on his way to school, and headed for the chicken house.

Feeding the chickens and gathering the eggs had become my job when I turned five. Father and Mother said there was always a job to be done when you lived on a farm and I was old enough to be considered a helper. Bob had been only too glad to hand the responsibility of the chickens over and move up the ladder to caring for the pigs.

In the early days, I wasn't very happy about chicken duty. I was frightened of the hens that all came running when I entered the henhouse with the feed bucket. They crowded about my legs and pecked at me with their sharp beaks. On my very first visit I had dropped the bucket of feed and run crying from the coop. But Mother wasn't one to allow anyone to quit. She took me back inside and rescued the feed bucket from the clucking hens. She sprinkled a few grains on the floor to divert the hens' attention as we filled the feed troughs. With the hens busily eating, I was able to quickly gather the eggs. Over the coming weeks I became an expert at feeding the chickens. To overcome my fear, I gave them names and personalities. There was Millie, who strutted just like the minister's wife; Alice, who was plain-looking just like her Great Aunt Cora; Ruth, from the Bible story; Jean, who was always last in line; and Ada, whose feathers were always ruffled like Mrs. Thompson up the road, and so the list went on. I never told my mother about the names, as she would have told me I was being disrespectful and that little girls shouldn't have such imaginations.

When I entered the chicken house this winter morning the clucking and rush of feathers toward me didn't ruffle me in the least. I threw out food, clearing a pathway for myself, and announced that Mother had a surprise for me and I needed their cooperation to finish my work quickly. In record time, the hens were eating, and gave up their eggs without protest.

When I arrived back indoors, the kitchen was sparkling clean and Mother was dressed in her town clothing. Father, whistling a Christmas carol, was standing at the porch sink, stripped to the waist, face lathered for a shave. A small suitcase sat open on the kitchen table. In a glance I realized it was packed with my things. Catching my look of surprise, Mother laughed.

"Come, June, be quick to change. You are off to visit your Aunt Drucie and Uncle Garnet and that new baby cousin in Summerside for a couple of days. It is your Christmas gift from us. Quick now, we need to catch the train at Miscouche."

A short time later, I sat between my parents on the train and couldn't believe my luck. I was going to stay in Summerside with my favourite aunt! Summerside was a whole different world from Central. There were streets lined with stores containing so much *stuff* that my eyes couldn't possibly see it all. In my aunt's apartment you could press a button on the wall and lights came on in the ceiling as though by magic. They even had a flush chamber pot and there were no chickens to feed. It was dreamlike to a country girl of five.

Aunt Drucie was my heroine. She was young and pretty and she lived in Summerside, and—best of all—she adored me. I had been concerned when Aunt Drucie got the new baby boy named Deric, but I need not have worried. I was still her favourite girl. Aunt Drucie was waiting at the station when the train pulled into Summerside. I ran from the train straight into her arms.

"Have you heard I am coming to stay with you?"

Aunt Drucie laughed. "A little elf told me about it, and I am most pleased. I have a whole list of things for us to do."

I said goodbye to my parents and, putting my hand in Aunt Drucie's, started off on a new adventure. We walked back to her apartment, which I was sure was really a doll's house. The rooms were so tiny and warm compared to the rambling farmhouse. There was no big kitchen range to pour warmth into the rooms or cook the food. Instead there were these strange looking radiators along the walls and a square stove in the kitchen that Aunt Drucie called the electric range. When she turned a knob, a red spot appeared on which to place a cooking pot.

A neighbour had kept Deric while Aunt Drucie went to meet me at the train. I couldn't believe how much the baby had grown. He was now a chubby little boy, who seemed glad to see me. When he settled for his nap, Aunt Drucie and I rearranged the furniture in the small living room to make way for the tree that Uncle Garnet was bringing home after work. I wasn't sure how he was going to find a tree in town—there were no woods to travel to and cut one down. Aunt Drucie explained you just *bought* a Christmas tree. It didn't sound like much fun to me but if that was how townspeople did it, it must be okay.

When Uncle Garnet came through the door with the tree it looked just like the tree at home except much smaller. But then, a doll-size house would need a smaller tree. I helped him set the tree in its stand while Aunt Drucie got the decorations out of storage. I had never seen ornaments for trees that looked anything like Aunt Drucie's. Hers were store-bought—nothing like Mother's home-made ones. Uncle Garnet put strings of lights on the tree. When he plugged the wire into a socket in the wall, the tree glowed with red, green, blue, yellow, and white. I stood spellbound.

It was the first tree I had seen with anything other than candles. Uncle Garnet said there was no risk of fire and they could leave the lights on for the whole evening. They placed each of the glass store-bought ornaments on the tree where they would sparkle and glitter from the rays of the lights. At last, Uncle Garnet placed a star at the top and Aunt Drucie turned out the ceiling light. Little Deric clapped his chubby hands together and squealed with delight. How could I ever go back to a country tree?

When I awoke the next morning, Aunt Drucie announced this was the day Santa Claus was coming to town. He would be arriving on a special train and then going to a department store to hear what the local children wanted for Christmas. I had never seen Santa in person before, let alone spoken to him, but I always sent a letter to the North Pole. Anticipation and fear filled my stomach: what would the real Santa be like?

When Aunt Drucie and I arrived downtown, the railway platform and station were filled with more children and adults than I had ever seen. They were all waving and shouting, "Here comes Santa Claus! Here comes Santa Claus!" I held my aunt's hand tightly.

Suddenly, in the distance, the train whistle began to blow and the engine could be heard slowing down on the tracks. I caught my first glimpse of Santa Claus standing at the door of the engine. My mouth dropped open in wonderment: he looked just like the Santa in magazine pictures. His suit was red and trimmed with real white fur that Aunt Drucie said was a gift from a polar bear. His boots reached his knees and were black as coal. But it was his eyes that held my attention. They were the bluest blue I had ever seen and he appeared to be looking right at me. He gave a merry laugh, jumped from the train, and walked through the train station, shouting "Ho, ho, ho" and "Merry Christmas to all!"

Santa went outside to a waiting horse and sleigh and was driven up Water Street to Holman's Department Store. The crowd rushed to follow him. Aunt Drucie explained that Santa would be seated in his large chair in Toyland. Each child would have a few moments to sit on his knee and tell him what he or she wished for for Christmas. The line was so long that I had plenty of time to think while I waited. I watched Santa gently pick up child after child and sit him or her on his knee. He asked each one the same question and I wondered how he could possibly remember their answers. But Aunt Drucie said there was no need to worry—Santa had a powerful memory and wasn't likely to ever forget a request. It was almost my turn when I finally made up my mind.

When I sat on Santa's knee I forgot to be nervous. I had a request that was much easier to tell Santa about in person than in a letter. I looked intently into his face.

"Santa, my aunt tells me you never forget a wish, so here is mine: I want a baby brother on Christmas Day just like the baby Jesus and my cousin Deric. I want him to be chubby and to laugh. I don't want one that cries and I don't want a sister. Is that clear, Santa?"

Santa was silent for what seemed like a long while. The children in the line began to fidget and people wondered what was happening. Finally he spoke in a soft voice only I could hear.

"Well now, June, that is a big request for Santa and I have to be truthful with you and tell you it's an order I can't deliver. Oh, I know people say Santa can do anything, but you see I don't make baby brothers in my workshop. They are a special order that come directly from God. Baby brothers, and yes, sisters too, take time to arrive for they are made with love and love takes time to grow. You'll have to be patient and have hope, for God will only send that baby boy if hope and love is there. Don't you forget that—and maybe you could ask *me* for a doll or a rubber ball."

I looked at Santa, disappointed with his answer but pleased with his truthfulness. Santa was like no other grownup I knew. When I got down from his knee Aunt Drucie asked what Santa and I had talked about. I told her that I asked for a doll and said no more. The rest of the conversation was my secret.

Since it was Saturday, Holman's stayed open late and it seemed everyone in town was there to shop. Aunt Drucie treated me to a chocolate sundae, and we walked through the store looking at all the delights. As darkness fell, we walked from one end of Water Street to the other to see the sparkling lights and store windows filled with Christmas scenes. I wondered if lights would ever come to the country. In a way I hoped they never would, for then the magic of town would disappear. As Aunt Drucie and I made our way home, we stopped in front of every house that had a tree in a window and made a wish for happiness in that home.

When I returned to the farm the next day, the chickens, Bob, Mother, and Father were all waiting for me. In the living room stood a big fir tree bare of shimmering lights, but dressed with handmade tokens of love. The kitchen range was pouring forth heat and suddenly I understood that the country had its own magic. This place had love within its walls. I had patience and I had hope.

On Christmas morning, I discovered Santa had left the doll I had asked for and he had even named her Molly. She was beautiful and the two of us became inseparable. Molly even learned to feed the chickens. It was two years before God delivered my baby brother. Santa was right: things grown with love did take time, but I had never given up hope. When he finally arrived, he was worth the wait.

A Winter Adventure on Skis

(1946)

Glenford MacLean of Southwest, Lot 16, shared this story with me one evening. He was certain he had nothing to tell until we began talking.

Over the span of my seventy-eight years, I have likely received hundreds of Christmas gifts. It's impossible to remember even a small number of them, including the most recent. The few I do remember stand out because they led to experiences that live on in my memory. I really don't think the boy can ever be extinguished in the body of the man. At least I hope not—boyhood for me was a time of freedom and wonder. There are many days I wish I could recapture the feeling. Sometimes I can, if I take a moment to sit and tell a story from my childhood.

I was the fourth and final child of my parents, Harold and Ella MacLean, born on August 2, 1936. My mother, a busy woman, determined she did not have time to visit the hospital—since it was a fine summer day and I was her fourth delivery—she decided to give birth at home. She took it all in stride and the routine of our household and farm hardly missed a beat. My parents named me Glenford.

The moment I found my feet, it was action time for my brother Allison and me. He was just two years older, but many people thought we were twins—we were inseparable. Allison and I looked for, and usually found, mischief. When our older siblings, Roger and Doreen, were left in charge of us, we kept them running. Doreen was ten when I was born and likely dismayed at the prospect of yet another brother.

I still remember the winter day we invaded Roger's bedroom and teased him to the point where he took after us. We were prepared. We ran down the hallway, threw open the window, and jumped to safety on the porch roof—or so we thought. We had not planned on Roger coming out through the window, forcing us into a new course of action: jumping off the roof into the snowbank below. It was all good for a laugh.

Our antics didn't just take place in the house, either: Allison and I sought out adventure in the barn loft, explored every inch of the farm, and thoroughly enjoyed being together.

My brother and I were always the first ones awake on Christmas morning. Since electric lights had not yet come to the community and we were not allowed to handle a lamp, we had to remain in bed until daybreak. Then, as quiet as mice, we would creep down the staircase and fix our eyes on the mantle where our clean wool socks hung. Eagerly, we would take the socks down and pull out the orange, apple, and few barley candies Santa had left inside. Then we would have to wait until Roger, Doreen, and our parents were ready to open the gifts sitting beneath the tree. In our home, Santa brought the stocking, but our parents gave the wrapped Christmas gifts.

Roger and Doreen always seemed to take their time getting ready on Christmas morning, causing Allison and me to grow more and more impatient and frustrated. In the end, though, the wait was worth it. The gifts we each received were always practical: if our skates were too small, we knew a new pair would be under the tree. Skating and pond hockey were our primary sources of entertainment during the long, cold winter months.

In the fall, as soon as the first skim of ice formed over Mick's Creek down by the river, all of the children would race there when school let out for the day. Many a time it was not safe, but that never stopped us. Anyone who fell through would only sink chest-deep in water and mud, and the rest of us would pull him or her out. The unlucky player would then hurry home, often a good half-mile across the fields, and dry out.

It was a learning experience for me to figure out what to ask for at Christmas. One of my early ideas was based on a tradition of my parents', who exchanged chocolates with my aunt and uncle each year. Though it was the same gift they gave and received, they each chose a different kind of the sweet treat. We children would be allowed one, possibly two, chocolates and I dreamed of having my very own box. The Christmas I was six, I asked Doreen if she might give me a box as a gift. I thought it was a pretty ingenious request. I would still get my gift from my parents and an additional gift from Doreen, who was a newly working teacher.

That Christmas Eve I developed a terrible toothache, and there was nothing that could be done that night. It was still causing me great misery on Christmas morning when, beneath the Christmas tree, I discovered the box of chocolates labelled *To Glenford, From Doreen*. The pain was so bad I could not eat even one of the candies I so longed for. My brothers said, since I was in no position to eat the chocolates, they would help me out. By the time I saw a dentist and had the tooth pulled, not one piece of chocolate remained.

The following Christmas I asked for, and received, a shovel. How my siblings and school friends laughed. Who would be stupid enough to ask for a shovel and create work for himself? All I will say is that it was a fine shovel and worked well.

By the time I was ten, I had learned a thing or two about asking for just the right gift. I cannot remember where Allison and I saw skis for the first time, but we quickly decided we had to have them. We put in our order with our parents and, lo and behold, there was a pair for each of us under the tree on Christmas morning, 1946.

In those days, winter came early and it came hard. Having no way to move snow from the farmyard other than by shovel, small mountains piled up quickly. In no time at all, snow covered the roofs of the lower farm buildings—perfect for sledding and downhill skiing.

That Christmas morning, the conditions were perfect. The hill created on the combined henhouse and pig barn was well over twelve feet and had a lovely firm crust that sparkled in the sunlight. Allison and I could not wait to try out our skis. As soon as the family gifts were open, we put on our outdoor clothing and rushed outside.

We climbed to the top of the roof-hill, strapped on the skis, and gripped the poles. Without a clue as to what we were doing, we propelled ourselves downward. We both managed to stay on our feet and by the time we came to a stop, we were more than two hundred yards away across the farmyard and into the treeline. Our shouts of unadulterated pleasure filled the air. I have no idea how many times we climbed up and skied down that hill. We certainly did not have to be encouraged to eat our Christmas dinner and we slept soundly that night.

In the following days, when we were not in school or doing chores, we were skiing. Soon, the hill was not challenging enough for us. We needed a bigger thrill, so we hatched a plan.

Our farm was a mixed operation: there were dairy cows, beef cattle, pigs, poultry, sheep, and horses. My father wintered his flock of sheep at the MacArthur Farm, approximately two miles down the New Road. Each day, he hauled feed in the pung sleigh with the driving horse, Jack.

The New Road was used heavily in winter as a shortcut from the opposite side of the Grand River. By crossing the frozen river and going over farm fields to the New Road, travellers could cut miles off their trips to Summerside. The regular traffic ensured New Road was packed down and made travel easy for a horse and sleigh. Allison and I determined it would be the ideal ski track.

We told Father we were willing to take on the extra chore of feeding the sheep at MacArthur Farm. Our father would have no reason to be suspicious of our offer, for we enjoyed the sheep and loved the lambs that had been born that spring.

There was one ram in particular that we loved to tease. He roamed freely about the farmyard and we thought it the greatest thing to stand in front of the barn door and get him worked up enough to charge us. The moment before he reached us, we would jump aside and he would run full force into the barn door. This caused us to howl with laughter and most days we could usually get him to do it several times before he caught on. However, he was not a helpless victim. He would often lay in wait until he saw us crossing the farmyard carrying pails of grain, and though we kept watch, he frequently succeeded in swooping in and head-butting one of us on the behind. We would be jolted forward or driven to the ground, but never seriously hurt.

The sheep provided the wool that made our blankets, socks, mittens, hats, and scarves and when they were sheared— after lambing in the spring—Allison and I were assigned to steadily turn the crank of the small machine that powered the shearer's clippers. It was hard work, but we never complained. We figured it would seem natural for us to take on more sheep-related responsibility. If he was suspicious of our eagerness, he never let on, and gladly passed over the chore.

When the sheep needed feeding, we loaded the grain and hay into the pung sleigh along with our skis and a long rope. We harnessed Jack, backed him into the traces, and set out onto the New Road. Once we made sure the coast was clear, I slipped on my skis, tied one end of the rope to the back of the sleigh, and firmly took hold of the opposite end. Allison would get settled in the driver's seat and wait for me to give the signal. Then, he would slap the reins and get the horse up to full speed as quickly as possible. This was not difficult for Jack, who loved to run...and had a mind of his own.

The horse had one time infuriated my mother, who, accompanied by Doreen, was driving him along the New Road heading for the village of Miscouche to catch the train. Jack veered off the road and onto my father's wood road, used for harvesting the winter firewood, and took off at full speed. By the time my mother finally brought Jack under control and got him turned around, and backtracked the distance they had covered, the train had long left the station. Yes, Jack loved to run and we were eager to give him his head. Whoever was driving basically just let Jack go and held onto the reins. Meanwhile, the skier at the end of the rope was having the trip of a lifetime.

I remember well the nervous excitement of waiting for the rope to go taut and the sudden jerk that pulled me forward as Jack took off. There was no way to control the horse's move-ment, and concentration had to be placed on staying upright and holding onto the rope. One moment I would be straight behind the sleigh with the spray of the snow whipping into my face, stinging it raw, and the next second I was veering widely to the left and up onto the banks of the road shoulder before bouncing off, back to the centre, and then out to the right to navigate that shoulder bank before coming back to the centre. The force of the wind whipped my breath away, yet somehow I could still laugh and shout out to go faster still. I doubt that Allison ever looked back once to see my fate.

When Allison would bring Jack to a stop in front of the sheep barn, I would go on by them and slowly glide to a stop. On the return trip we would change positions and I drove while Allison skied. We would stop short of the home farm and Jack always cooperated as though in on the secret. He, too, enjoyed our adventure. We never gave a thought to the possibilities of something going wrong, and thus they never did. We were totally in the moment—enjoying the pleasure to the fullest. In hindsight, I am sure our parents knew what we were up to, but they never interfered nor do I imagine did they worry. They let it be—and it was great.

Allison and I used those skis until they could be used no more. We probably enjoyed them for at least six winters and we never grew tired of them. One day, they simply disappeared, and we moved on to creating new memories. In later years, I went downhill skiing on a real ski hill with my ten-year-old niece. By then, I had forgotten how to relax and hold my body in the position of a skier. I came down the hill in a crouched position and my wife heard people, watching through the windows of the clubhouse, say, "Who is that old man out there skiing with that little girl?" That ended my skiing career. If only those people had seen me skiing behind Jack on the treasured skis found under a childhood Christmas tree, they would have watched in awe and clapped with glee, while shouting, "Faster, young man!"

The Christmas Concert

(1946)

THE IDEA FOR THIS STORY CAME FROM A CONVERSATION HELD OVER LUNCH WITH JUNE HUTCHINSON MacLEAN. SOMETIMES IT SEEMS AS IF THE CHRISTMAS CONCERT IS AS SPECIAL AS CHRISTMAS ITSELF.

The dancing sunlight forced June's eyes open. It made the frost on her windowpane glitter like the diamond chips in her Great-Aunt Pearl's broach. As she watched the sun's performance she suddenly remembered—today was the day she had long anticipated. It had finally arrived!

June threw back the heavy quilts and leaped to the floor, for once not minding the winter cold of her farmhouse bedroom. She skipped across the room and down the stairs. On winter days, Mother would take June's clothing down to warm by the kitchen stove where she was allowed to wash and dress. There would only be her mother in the kitchen, for her older brother and father would still be outside finishing the morning chores. The smell of baking bread wafted from the oven. June had helped her mother set the yeast sponge the previous night. The porridge was bubbling and Mother was making tea when June burst into the kitchen.

"Isn't it the greatest morning!" she shouted.

Mother gave a slow smile as she crossed to the wood box and carried another log to the kitchen range. The sparks from the fire crackled when she dropped it in.

"And what would have you in such a fine mood this morning, June Margaret?"

June stopped short in the midst of stripping off her flannel nightshirt, surprise and shock registering on her small face.

"Mother! You couldn't have forgotten the day of the school Christmas concert—it's my first one ever."

Mother laughed aloud. "Calm yourself, June. I haven't forgotten, but there is a lot to be done before the big moment tonight so hurry and get ready for school. Miss MacArthur will need everyone's help today. We'll go over your part while I braid your hair."

June's part in the Christmas concert was to give the welcome. That role was always given to a grade one student and when Miss MacArthur had given it to her, June nearly cried with excitement. Her brother, Bob, had mercilessly teased her, saying everyone knew the best parts went to the teacher's pets. June protested: she had gotten the part because she had a good memory, could speak loudly, and looked angelic. She would have been dismayed to know Miss MacArthur had chosen her because she was the one child in grade one who had not yet lost any teeth and could articulate clearly.

Quickly, June washed her face and hands and began to dress. She pulled on her heavy underwear and wool stockings. Today, all was right with the world—she wouldn't even complain about those itchy homemade stockings. She sat by the fire while Mother combed and braided her long black hair. Usually this was June's favourite time of day, but this morning she was anxious to get going.

"June," Mother scolded, "if you can't stay still it will take twice the time and hurt twice as much. Now sit nicely and recite your welcome."

The rehearsal wasn't really necessary. June knew her piece by heart, and planned to make her beloved teacher and parents proud...and maybe show her brother a thing or two. June had waited for what seemed like forever for a part in the school Christmas concert. Since the age of four she had watched Bob perform, and in her eyes it was always a magical evening.

Her only disappointment with the concert was last year's Santa. The week before the concert she had seen Santa Claus at Holman's Department Store in Summerside. He was just as Santa should be—a jolly man with a round face, long white beard, glasses, and a voice so gentle it was impossible to be frightened of him. She had climbed on his knee and earnestly recited her wish list. He had solemnly told her he would try his best and whatever was under the tree on Christmas morning would have been placed there with great love. The Santa who arrived at the Christmas concert was too loud and boisterous.

"That can't be Santa—it must be one of his sons," June had announced to her mother. When the people seated around them laughed, June hid her face in her father's chest. She still saw nothing funny about the matter. But that was last year; she was hopeful her Holman's Store Santa would attend this year's concert.

Finally, Mother finished June's braids and helped her into her outdoor clothing. As she did every day, Mother instructed Bob to watch out for his sister on the walk to school. It was early when June and her brother arrived at the one-room schoolhouse, their cheeks glowing from the brisk walk and the frosty air. They quickly hung their coats and stowed their boots, and rushed to join the other students. Each and every child was smiling and eager; there was a lot of work to be done and not much time. The large fir tree—which the older boys had cut down the previous afternoon—lay waiting on the floor. The boys began nailing the stump to a board that would be nailed to the floor at the front of the schoolroom in the left corner.

Once the tree was in place the younger children began to decorate it with paper angels and bells, apples, gingerbread men, ropes of popcorn and cranberries, and tinsel. A beautiful store-bought star, for which the children had each donated a nickel, topped the tree. Mrs. Miller, a parent always eager to help out, arrived with bags of running spruce to decorate the windows and door wells. The smell of greenery soon filled the school. Students hung quilts over stretched wire to enclose the teacher's raised platform as a stage and pushed the desks against the wall to make room for the audience chairs.

After lunch, Miss MacArthur held a quick practise and then dismissed the children early so they could complete their after-school chores before returning for the concert. June and her brother raced to reach home first. Bob split wood for kindling and June carried it into the house. She filled the woodbox while Bob went to drive the cattle and horses down to the brook for a drink. June set the table for Mother and rushed through her own supper. She had the dishes cleared before Father even finished his tea, and rushed off for her bath. Once again, Mother brushed and braided her hair beside the warm kitchen range. June was ready to get dressed.

She stopped short when she entered her bedroom. Lying across her bed was a beautiful red crushed-velvet dress with a white lace collar. Mother came up the stairs behind her and stood in the doorway, a smile on her face.

"I made it for your special night, June," she said. "The red will look beautiful with your black braids, and the white lace collar perfectly matches your white stockings"

Mother carefully placed the dress over June's head so as not to untidy her hair. June slipped her arms into the sleeves, and as the dress floated downward and fitted to her body she felt the softness of the material against her skin. She smoothed down the crushed velvet with her hands, unable to describe how it felt beneath her fingertips. When Mother finished fastening the buttons, June stood in front of the mirror looking at her reflection. She smiled. She was the luckiest girl. She heard Bob rushing down the steps and she knew it was time to go.

Father was waiting at the kitchen door with the horse and sleigh. Everyone climbed in for the short trip to school, cuddled beneath the buffalo robes. Father slapped the reins and the horse, Spark, was off through the deep snow. The sound of his bells jingling in the crisp, clear air was perfect as the sky filled with sparkling stars. Father said each person had his or her own star. Looking into the vastness of the heavens, June wondered which one was hers. She prayed her star would watch over her performance tonight and help her shine.

Numerous sleighs were entering the schoolyard, dropping their passengers at the door before crossing to the MacGregor barn where the horses could stay warm for the duration of the concert. People called Christmas greetings back and forth across the yard as they entered the schoolhouse. Stanley, who was in his final year at the school, was stationed in the porch collecting the ticket fee. The proceeds of the concert went to the Junior Red Cross.

June stood inside the door and drank in the sights and sounds. The schoolhouse was transformed with the soft glow of the gas lights. The Christmas decorations looked brilliant and warmth radiated from the stove. Seats were filling up quickly, and the air was filled with happy chatter. Some of the women were handing over bags of homemade fudge to be sold at intermission, and June's mouth watered at the thought of the sugary treat.

Miss MacArthur caught June's eye and began beckoning her to join the students by the stage. The spell was broken and butterflies began to dance in her stomach. Then, before she knew it, she was standing before the audience in her new red dress delivering the welcome so that each person felt they had been personally invited to the concert. When she finished, she found the faces of her parents in the crowd and saw their smiles of pride.

As the audience began to clap, June flushed a deep red to match her dress. She curtsied and exited the stage. Now, she could relax and enjoy the rest of the concert. The recitations, carols, and skits seemed to go by in an instant.

Soon the door at the back of the school was opening, and Santa entered. The crowd—and June—watched him closely as he made his way to the stage. To her delight, he looked just like the Santa from Holman's; the real one had found the time to come to her concert! Santa called forth each child individually and gave him or her a gift. As she accepted hers, June leaned forward to kiss his cheek and whisper her thanks in his ear. The twinkle in his deep blue eyes as he winked thrilled the little girl and filled her heart with love. He was indeed the real Santa.

Finally the evening, so long anticipated, drew to a close. June stood outside the school with Mother and Bob, waiting for Father to come with the horse and sleigh. She called out, "Merry Christmas!" to everyone who walked by. Soon she was snuggled under the buffalo robes as Spark followed her father's commands and headed for home. She lay back on the soft straw and watched the night sky, searching for a glimpse of the red-suited man who had brought a perfect ending to her perfect evening.

The Bells

(1948)

THIS IS A THIRD STORY FROM JUNE HUTCHINSON MACLEAN.
ON A HOLIDAY VISIT TO HER HOME, I NOTICED A BEAUTI-
FUL SET OF HORSE BELLS DISPLAYED WITH THE CHRISTMAS
DECORATIONS. AS SOON AS I INQUIRED ABOUT THEM I KNEW
I HAD ANOTHER CHRISTMAS STORY.

I was eight years old during Christmas 1948, and I looked forward to the day with unrivalled anticipation. "Christmas is
for children," I often heard adults say, and heartily agreed. The
festive season of '48 was to leave an impression on my young
soul that deeply influenced me in the coming years.

The hard lean years of the war were finally behind us.
Neither cash nor supplies were as scarce, and some aspects
of new technology were coming to our rural community. The
previous summer Father had purchased both a tractor and a
car, and he marvelled at the increased productivity and how
quickly he could scoot to town in the car. Unlike so many
farmers in the community, he had refused to sell the horses.
He had his reasons. He explained that the car was not as

efficient in the snow and would spend the winter stuck at the end of our long farm lane, perhaps waiting up to a week for a plough. He couldn't chance being without dependable transportation.

Mother agreed, making it unnecessary for Father to voice the real reason: his love and loyalty to the Percheron horses, Tim and Spark. Mother was well aware that he loved to harness one or the other to the sleigh and drive us children to school in the early morning or to a pond hockey game at night. She knew how much time he spent brushing their silky coats and talking to them about everything from the price of farm produce to current events. Mother understood the continued need of the horses, and, unbeknownst to any of the family, she began to make plans.

Mother started preparing for Christmas in the springtime. To ensure she would have the necessary money for the holiday, she purchased young roosters and turned them into capons to sell at the Christmas market. She also picked for herself a calf from the beef herd to fatten for sale in the fall.

Then, come late fall, when Mother sat at the kitchen table with the Eaton's catalogue and order form, we made sure she knew our Christmas wishes. One day in December as I prepared to leave for school, Mother handed me her order form and money wrapped in cloth to place in the mailbox at the end of the lane. The mailman would make sure the order and money found its way to Eaton's and sometime later, he would return to deliver the parcel. Doing business in this manner was a common practice for country people who trusted the mailman.

Several days after the order was sent, Mother told me she had a new assignment for me: when coming home from school I was not to take the shortcut across the fields, but rather follow the road, collect the mail, and bring it directly home each day. She said if Father was in the barnyard watering the cattle, I was to ignore him and head directly to the house. Her request was unusual—Father usually got the mail before he came in for supper—but I offered no argument, for it was Santa season.

As December advanced, Mother's step quickened. The aroma of white and dark fruitcake, cranberry loaf, raisin butter tarts, mincemeat pies, and sugar cookies would greet us when we entered the kitchen after school. Mother was forever telling Father not to over-stoke the wood range and burn any of her creations.

One morning Mother informed me that Santa had awoken her from a deep sleep the night before to explain that Mrs. Santa was overburdened with work. He was requesting Mother's assistance in knitting me a sweater for Christmas morning and was dropping off the yarn and pattern. Of course, Mother agreed to help. She saw no reason to risk knitting the sweater the wrong size and measured me up then and there. I was excited because the sweater buttoned up the front and had a pattern of bears walking from front to back. It never occurred to me that perhaps the element of surprise was now gone.

I already knew what several of my gifts would be. My Aunt Katherine was making me a hooked mat to stand on when I got dressed on cold winter mornings. The pattern was Poppa, Momma, and Baby Bear each holding steaming bowls of porridge. Last Christmas, Santa had left me a doll so I was pretty confident this year he would bring clothing for her. If the doll's dress was made from the same material as one of my own, there was a simple explanation: Mrs. Claus and Mother both shopped at Holman's Department Store in Summerside.

After a week or so, I was getting discouraged picking up the mail: it was never anything more than the newspaper, and I had to walk an extra half-mile from school. But one day I saw a parcel wedged into the snowbank beside the mailbox and I couldn't have been any more excited than if Santa himself had appeared before me. When I picked up the box and started to run up the lane, something within rattled slightly. Father was just herding the cattle from the barn to the water trough and I avoided him without difficulty. As soon as she saw the box, Mother took it and marched straight upstairs, not allowing us to see what was inside.

To an eight year old, it seemed Christmas Eve would never arrive. But, as dawn eventually follows night, it came. When we arrived home from church and were preparing Santa's snack, I witnessed my mother placing a parcel under the tree. For reasons I could not explain, I felt sure it was a special gift for me. I scurried off to bed, willing morning to come quickly.

Christmas Day dawned clear and brilliant from the fresh-fallen snow that came overnight. Father and the boys hurried through the barn chores while I helped Mother in the kitchen. Before making breakfast, she prepared the large chicken and goose. She stuffed them full of dressing and coated their skins with rich farm butter. She popped them in the hot oven of the range, and when the boys came in from the barn the odour of roasting fowl filled the air.

The moment the breakfast dishes were cleared, we gathered around the tree and Mother handed out gifts. Santa's sweater for me was wrapped in brown paper with a red ribbon. My eager hands tore it open and I gave a squeal of delight at the finished product. I was quite sure Mrs. Claus would be pleased with Mother's work. I was more than happy, though, that it was Mrs. Claus herself who made my doll clothes. My brothers opened their gifts of checkers, mittens, socks, and pyjamas.

It was now down to the one mysterious gift under the tree. Mother, with a mischievous smile, picked up the parcel and handed it to Father. Surprised, he reached to take it from her outstretched hand.

"Merry Christmas, Bill," she whispered.

They smiled at each other. None of us spoke as we watched our father gently turn the box over and over. Slowly, he began to remove the ribbon that held the brown paper in place. I studied my father's face as he stripped away the paper to reveal four beautiful brass horse bells mounted on polished leather. It was a mixture of shock, delight, wonder, and pure love that filled his eyes as he looked from the bells to my mother and back again. His voice shook as he offered his thanks. In that moment, I understood the beauty of giving in love and the art of receiving with gratitude.

The bells brought my father years of joy. They hung in our kitchen long after Spark stopped hauling the sleigh and creating music in the winter air. Upon his death, my father left his precious bells to me and each time I hear their sound, I am once again a witness to love.

Christmas from the Ashes

(1949)

THIS STORY CAME FROM EDNA CAMERON SHEEN IN 2011.
EDNA LEFT PRINCE EDWARD ISLAND AS A TEENAGER TO PUR-
SUE A CAREER IN ONTARIO, BUT HER ISLAND ROOTS REMAIN
STRONG AND SHE OFTEN RETURNS HOME.

In November, I returned to the place of my childhood. I was seeking the sense of calm I was certain Prince Edward Island would bring. I also had a sense of urgency to visit my cousins who, like me, were growing older, their steps slower and more weighted with the passing of time.

We enjoyed a simple supper made complete by fresh apple pie and tea served in china cups. I pushed back from my cousin's table and joined the others in comfortable chairs by the wood stove. My body relaxed as though my very cells were recalling old times. As I embraced the feeling, my cousin asked if we could recount a memorable Christmas. I turned and looked out the window at the moonlit farmyard and it was as if the years melted away. Suddenly, it was 1949 and I was a young woman of eighteen.

A few years earlier, when I was fifteen, my stepfather had purchased Sharp's General Store in Tyne Valley. It was nestled at the bottom of the hills in the little village and fronted the main road, just feet from the riverbank. No matter the season, the view from the large plate-glass windows was beautiful. The two-storey building housed the store, a small library, a storage space, and two apartments. Dad (that is what I called my stepfather), Mother, our two dogs, Lady and Rags, and I made one of the apartments our home.

Dad stocked a wide variety of goods in his general store. Customers could purchase clothing, footwear, kitchen gadgets, kerosene, nails, dry goods, and so much more. I still remember the large wheel of cheddar cheese, procured from the cheese factory in Arlington, which he would cut and wrap in brown paper tied with string for his customers. But it was the candy counter that drew me like a magnet. I was an expert at snatching the penny candy by quietly opening the sliding door of the display case and slipping in my hand. The soft-centered creams were always my favourite, followed by hard barley candy. People came and went through the double doors, the bell announcing their arrival and departure, and I enjoyed watching the social and business exchanges from the background. I might even admit to enjoying my exchanges with the young man who worked there.

I finished school at age sixteen and, after six weeks at Prince of Wales College in Charlottetown, I assumed the teaching position at Birch Hill School. Though only a few miles from the valley, it was too far to travel on a daily basis so I boarded with my aunt and uncle in the community and travelled home on weekends. I always enjoyed coming home to the familiar smells and sounds.

Growing up in a small rural community in the forties had not always been easy for me. I had a loving family—I never doubted that—and any time I visited extended family I was treated as though I was their own. But I, like the community that surrounded me, never forgot that my biological father was not part of my upbringing. I doubted I could reach my full potential if I remained at home. My aunt, who had remained single and became a nurse, encouraged me to follow her footsteps. She thought Montreal would be the ideal place for me to get my training. Somehow, I found the courage to follow her advice and in January 1949, at age eighteen, I boarded the train for the big city. To this day I dislike trains—even the sight of one stirs up the fear and loneliness that comes from being carried away from everything you know and love.

The Royal Victoria Hospital in Montreal became my school, my workplace, and my home. While homesickness gripped me at times, I drew comfort from the other Maritime girls who were in the same situation. The days were filled with learning and quickly turned into weeks, which turned into months, and before I knew it, it was the first of December. I was heading home for the first time in eleven months. When the train pulled into Summerside, I shook with excitement and was full of thanks that my uncle, who collected me at the station, headed straight for the valley.

When I arrived home, I bypassed the store and went through the back entrance to the apartment seeking the welcome of my mother and my dog, Lady, who missed me dreadfully. She had disappeared the day I left and was later found under my bed with her head in my slipper, whimpering. I was not disappointed, for both were there to greet me and soon it was as though I had never left.

Even living so close to the store with its comings and goings, Tyne Valley seemed very quiet compared to Montreal. Time flew as we made preparations for Christmas, visited relatives and friends, and enjoyed church and school concerts. When I had spare time I helped in the store, which was bustling with people preparing for the holiday.

All of a sudden, it was Christmas morning. While I might have had a year of nurse's training under my belt, I was still as excited as a small child waiting to discover what Santa had brought. I was not disappointed. In the cozy warmth of the small apartment, my parents took a small box from beneath the Christmas tree and presented it to me. I tore away the wrapping paper to reveal a small jeweller's box. Inside was the most beautiful ring: two turquoise stones nestled around a pearl. The stunning gift took my breath away. I slipped the ring on my finger to find that it fit perfectly.

As I sat admiring my gift, Dad reached under the tree once again and pulled out another package. This time, he presented it to my mother. She opened it to find a string of pearls. She loved pearls, and the look that passed between them told me he could have given her no greater gift. But, unlike me, she tenderly laid the necklace back in its case and placed it under the tree. Christmas Day, which we spent together as a family, came and went.

On Boxing Day, I was eager to visit my Aunt Jessie and Uncle Gordon and spend time with my cousins, Jean and Glen, who were more like sisters to me. I gladly walked the three miles to be with them and my parents came that evening for supper. While we were enjoying that festive meal, a knock came at the door. It was a neighbour, Seaman Ford, who had received a call that Dad's store was on fire. The mood turned from festive to fearful. Dad, telling Mom and myself to stay put, jumped in the car and headed for the valley.

Well, Mom might have been willing to do as she was told, but not me. Grabbing our outdoor clothing, my cousin Glen and I began to run for the valley. When we arrived at the bottom of the hill there was no store—once enveloped in flames, the wooden structure had burned quickly. Nothing had been saved. When my father relayed this to my mother, they both began to cry. But one small thing had been saved: on my finger was the Christmas ring and there it remains to this day.

Dad had not believed in insurance and there was no way to raise the store from the ashes. I faced returning to Montreal at the end of the month without a suitcase or clothes to go in it. More importantly, my experience card (needed to qualify to write my exams) had also burned. But the spirit of Christmas filled the hearts of the people of Tyne Valley and the surrounding communities. In a short time, they gathered gifts and raised money. The gift I remember most was the pretty pink tam Mrs. Williams knitted. Thankfully my Montreal nursing instructors showed compassion and issued me a new experience card.

When I boarded the train to Montreal, leaving my parents to put their lives back together, I did not know that it would be my last Christmas in the valley with family and friends. In the years that have come and gone since, I only returned to the Island once for Christmas with my parents, who called Charlottetown home by then. But the Christmas of 1949 comes to life in my memory when I think of my Prince Edward Island home.

The Spirit of an Evergreen

(1950)

EDWARD CLARK TOLD THIS STORY AS HE RELAXED IN HIS KITCHEN IN BELMONT, PEI, IN MARCH 2015. HIS WIFE, RUBY, OFFERED A COMMENT HERE AND THERE, AND SERVED DELICIOUS HOMEMADE CINNAMON ROLLS. IN THE WARMTH OF THE FIRE, THE YEARS SLIPPED AWAY.

Is there a greater thing of beauty than a simple Christmas tree decorated to show its finery? Think of it: a tree, sacrificed in winter for the festive transformation of a home, which somehow instils in the hearts of its occupants a sense of wonder and hidden promise. What could hold more beauty than that?

As a boy, growing up in Belmont, Prince Edward Island, I dreamed of having a tree grace our family home and bring the excitement of the season into our midst. My younger sister,

Thelma, had the same desire, but because our Christmas was celebrated at the home of my mother's parents we had no tree of our own.

My maternal grandparents, Edward and Blanche Miller, (Pups and Mum), were hard-working and generous people who believed in church and community. They enjoyed prosperity from their farm on Lyle Road in the settlement of Central. Grandfather expanded his mixed farm to invest in silver black foxes and it paid handsomely. He built Blanche a fine four-corner-square house, or, as they are known on the Island, a fox house. Life was good.

Their family consisted of them and their twin girls, Maisy and Gladys. My grandmother and her daughters were very attached to each other.

Maisy, the twin who would become my mother, went into nurse's training as a young woman. Though she was a natural caregiver, she did not complete the course and returned home to the family farm. I was never told why, for people did not speak of such things, but I have often wondered if her decision was based on homesickness for her parents.

The man who would become my father, Ivan Clark, was returning to the community of his youth at the same time. A few years previously when Ivan's brother, Earl, had returned from the Great War, the two joined the Northwest Mounted Police on a three-year contract and headed west. Ivan patrolled the streets of Vancouver and Kamloops on the back of a fine steed, and thought it a reasonable life. That is, until he was told he would be transferred to the northern wilderness, where one of his friends and fellow Mounties had mentally succumbed to the months of being alone in isolation. He decided to resign and headed home to PEI. He bought a farm about a half-mile down the road from Edward and Blanche, and began calling on Maisy. Ivan's mother, however, had other plans for her son and was heard to say, "There will be white crows flying before they'll be married."

Even so, the wedding soon took place. Within a year my brother, Leigh, was born. While Ivan was at work on the farm, Maisy put her training to good use and carried out nursing duties in homes throughout the community. My grandmother looked after Leigh when Mother worked and he grew more and more attached to her. One night, when Leigh was two or three years old, he would not stop crying so my father took him to his grandparents where he was immediately soothed. There he stayed to be raised by them, and somehow no one ever questioned the arrangement. Leigh was six years old when I was born in 1932, and though we knew we were brothers, we were not close and we never lived under the same roof.

I, in turn, was six years old when my sister was born in 1938. My father named her Thelma, after an old girlfriend he had known in his Mountie days. He had returned home with the pictures and names of ten women in his little book. Thelma and I developed a close bond and we shared in the mischief of childhood that still brings a twinkle to my eye and a smile to my lips. We also shared the disappointment of never having our own Christmas tree. Since we went to our grandparents' home, my mother never placed a Christmas decoration in her own simple farmhouse, no matter how much we children begged.

As was tradition, my grandparents' beautifully crafted home was decorated just prior to the big day itself. The women twisted together green and red streamers and strung them across the dining room ceiling from the four corners, and a deep-red bell was suspended over the centre of the dining room table. The Christmas colours were in sharp contrast to the rich wood grain of the Douglas fir walls. The pocket doors at the end of the dining room were pushed open during the Christmas season to reveal the seldom-seen front room, which housed the precious tree.

Three weeks prior to Christmas, Pups would go alone to the fifty-acre woods at the back of the farm and pick out what he thought was the perfect tree. Then, on Christmas Eve, he would go back and cut it down, drag it home, and set it up in the corner by the window that faced the road. Mum Blanche decorated the tree with glass icicles, silver tinsel, and beautiful, fragile, hand-painted glass balls. For fear of fire they never placed candles on the tree, but the lamps throughout the room reflected the colours and shimmer. When Thelma and I would first lay eyes on the tree on Christmas Day, it was a sight to behold.

In our own home on Christmas morning, Thelma and I always awoke before dawn. It never mattered how early we arrived in the kitchen, our father was always up ahead of us and had the fire burning brightly in the kitchen range to knock the chill off the frigid air. The hay, which I had put out on Christmas Eve for Santa's reindeer, would be gone. Since we had no tree, Santa Claus left our stockings on the oven door. It took mere seconds to dig out the apple, orange, and barley candy animal suckers. Curiously, I often found a brick in my stocking as well—I came to discover our hired man, Pres Winchester, placed it there as a joke. Our other gifts would be found under the tree at our grandparents' home.

We would rush to do up the morning chores, have breakfast, get dressed, and head for Mum and Pup's, where Leigh and our cousins would greet us. My mother's twin, Gladys, and her family always came from Charlottetown for Christmas. The dinner, served at noon, was roasted goose with all the trimmings, followed by fresh plum pudding. It was always delicious and our only complaint was the slight we children sometimes felt if required to sit at the small table because the dining room table was full.

As soon as we finished eating, we moved to the living room to open gifts, leaving the dishes until later. Clothing was more plentiful than toys, so we children often found this tradition rather disappointing. Perhaps that is why the one year I received a spinning top and Thelma received a bubble wand has stayed so clearly in my mind—as does the fact that I accidentally broke her bottle of bubble mixture.

Christmas evening at Mum and Pup's was a fun time. Their friends, the Campbells, arrived to play cards and we children played hide-and-seek from the bottom floor to the attic. The floor furnace radiated heat throughout the house and we took advantage of it. We were even so bold as to empty the drawers in the den, filled with the home-remedy products of the Rawleigh salesman who stayed overnight at my grandparents when he was in the Lot 16 area. Those drawers proved to be the perfect hiding place for a small child.

Some Christmases we stayed overnight at Mum and Pup's and enjoyed every moment of it, but still there remained that underlying sadness of not having a tree of our own at home. As I grew older, I became one of the boys responsible for cutting the Christmas trees for the school and church. We took the responsibility seriously and did our best to select trees that would make everyone ooh and aah. I longed for the opportunity to cut a tree for home.

When I was seventeen, a man named Jimmy Higgins walked approximately two miles through the back fields of his farm to the Lyle Road and knocked on my father's door. Years before, Jimmy's only son, Elton, had declared that he wanted to become a doctor instead of taking over the family farm. Jimmy refused to put him through medical school, hoping to keep him home. That had not deterred young Elton, and after serving as a pilot in the Second World War, he obtained his medical degree. He eventually moved to the United States to pursue his career.

Jimmy was now in his seventies and his wife was sick with consumption. He wanted my father to buy his farm, which fronted on Belmont Road. Another farm near Mum and Pup's was said to be coming on the market and Mother wanted to purchase that one.

To me, the Higgins farm was very desirable; I had ridden by it either on my bicycle or horse numerous times and admired the stately hip-roof barn with an ell for additional space. Compared to the two small barns on our farm, the Higgins structure was a modern dairy barn. It had a track that ran right through the loft, which allowed workers to drop hay into different built-in chutes that placed the fodder right in front of the cows. There was also a large water tank that gravity-fed the individual water bowls. They were genius, time-saving inventions. As if that was not enough, the barn even had a ventilation system.

Even their farmhouse was of better quality than our current home and had a wonderful feature—one of the three telephones in all of Belmont. Neighbours tried to discourage my father from buying the farm out of fear of consumption. That scared me, but not my father. He was ready to expand his farming operation, for I had finished my formal education the previous year and was now farming with him full-time. His plan was to hold onto his current property for the land and buy the Higgins farm to live in. He made arrangements to borrow the money and a new chapter in our lives began.

We moved in May 1950 and the very next day I had the Junior Farmer's Club over to tour the barn. The smile on my face went ear to ear as I listened to the compliments of my peers. The family quickly settled in. Our new house had an impressive kitchen, which turned out to be big enough to hold dances attended by both young and old. My mother hosted card parties as an enterprising way to raffle off ducks and increase her profit margin. Thelma was the only one with a complaint, for at first she missed her old school. Soon enough, however, she met new friends and had a change of heart.

The summer and fall of 1950 passed in the blink of an eye and before we knew it, the Christmas season was upon us. It was our first holiday on the new farm and Thelma and I were intent on starting a new tradition. We were determined to have our very own Christmas tree. With trepidation but determination, we stood before our mother and declared that a new home for our family deserved its very own tree. I will never know if it was because of our stance, or perhaps her personal desire, but she did not argue.

Though Thelma and I had always looked forward to Christmas, our excitement was unmatched this year. We had no decorations for a tree so we pooled our money and bought glass icicles, which cost twenty-five cents per package. Thelma took on the time-consuming job of stringing cranberries to make colourful garlands and she cut out scenes from old Christmas cards and threaded them to hang as ornaments. Then we headed to the woods to find ourselves an evergreen. Since we would still be going to Mum and Pup's for Christmas Day, we decided to put our tree up three days early so we could enjoy it to the fullest.

There is something spiritual about walking through woods in early winter. The silence speaks to you, as though you're holding a conversation with the forest inside your head. The interruptions—the sound of snow falling from boughs, a bird's call, squirrels scurrying from tree to tree—are welcome. You almost observe them in an enlightened manner that says we are all one and at home in this sacred place. In this wonderful setting, Thelma and I picked out our tree. The sound of my axe resounded through the woods and was carried in the wind. We each had a sense of contentment as we began our journey home with the treasure.

I sawed straight across the bottom of the tree and nailed it to a board. Together, Thelma and I carried it into the house and put it in the living room next to the window. The warmth of the parlour stove helped carry the smell of the tree throughout the house. Thelma placed the decorations carefully. When she was finished, we stood and looked at the fulfillment of a dream years in the making. It was more than a Christmas tree: it was about finding a voice and having it heard. It was about knowing dreams can come true.

By commercial standards, our humble tree would not have been considered a thing of beauty. But in our eyes, there had never been a better one. Now that we were growing older, Santa did not stop at our house on Christmas Eve anymore. Something goes out of Christmas when he no longer comes, but we had our own tree and that made it possible to embrace and enjoy the family celebration at my grandparents' home. Thelma received a beautiful cradle for her doll, handmade by Uncle Eldon. It was a Christmas to remember.

In the coming year of 1951, I felt the need to venture from the safety of my parents' farm and discover the world. I joined the Royal Canadian Navy and trained at Cornwallis in Nova Scotia before serving in Victoria, British Columbia. A year and a half later, I was ordered to return to Halifax. Shortly thereafter, my father injured his arm and needed me to come home and help him on the farm. I finally understood my connection to the place and appreciated its value. I was discharged from the Navy and returned to my roots.

Five years later in 1958, I married my wife, Ruby, and we lived with my parents in their home. After a time, my parents decided to turn the farmhouse over to us and bought a smaller home for themselves. Thelma now had a life and family of her own, and our Christmas traditions were changing.

When our first of three daughters, Colleen, was born, I wanted her to experience Christmas morning in her own home. We devised a schedule: Ruby's parents would join us for the noontime meal, and we would go to Mum and Pup's in the evening. Placing a Christmas tree in our living room became a treasured family tradition and our inventory of decorations grew steadily. It is only in the past several years that Ruby and I, now great-grandparents ourselves, have admitted that an artificial tree is now easier. Though the evergreen scent no longer fills the house, even a decorated artificial tree has its beauty.

When December arrives, I often sit in my living room and stare at the current year's tree. I find myself thinking of all the trees I've seen over eighty-some years and reflect on the many changes. I feel nothing but satisfaction, for I have experienced the love of a family gathered round a Christmas tree.

The Girls
Select the Tree

(1963)

THIS STORY IS DRAWN FROM MY OWN CHILDHOOD EXPERI‑
ENCE OF GOING FOR THE CHRISTMAS TREE WITH FAMILY AND
OUR BELOVED HORSE, FANNY.

She awoke knowing something special was planned for today. Then Marlene remembered. It was the day to get the Christmas tree! She threw back the quilts, her feet barely touching the ice-cold floor as she ran to the window. Using her hand and warm breath, she made a circle in the middle of the frosty glass to see outside. She squinted from the brilliance of the sunlight reflecting on the crystal-white snow. The day was perfect for going to the woods to find a tree. She gathered her clothing and raced downstairs to the kitchen to dress before the warm wood stove.

Mother and Father had been up for hours and having lit the fire in the big stove, the chill of winter had quickly dissipated from the room. Marlene's two older sisters were eating their porridge at the kitchen table.

"Come on, slowpoke," Christine muttered, "We've got a tree to get."

"Let her be," commanded her older sister, Debbie, "We can't go anywhere until Mother and Father have completed the barn chores."

Dressed and toasty warm, Marlene reached for the toasting grill and held a thick slab of homemade bread over the open flame of the stove.

"It's a perfect day to get the Christmas tree," she said. "I hope Mother and Father won't take long."

After finishing their breakfast, the girls cleaned the kitchen and waited in front of the window for their parents. Shortly, they saw their father come out of the barn leading Fanny; he was backing the gentle mare into the traces of the sleigh. This was their cue. The girls started putting on layers of winter clothing. They took their boots, warm and dry, from behind the stove. They donned their snow pants and coats and took their mittens, hats, and scarves from the warming closet of the stove. Within minutes, the girls were ready to travel.

Mother came into the kitchen and after a few minutes of rattling about in the pantry, she, too, was ready to leave. They all climbed into the back of the sleigh and, once seated, Father slapped the reins: Fanny was off through the snow. Fortunately, the snowfall covering wasn't deep and Fanny made good time towards the woods at the back of the farm. The girls sang carols and occasionally reached over the sides of the sleigh to scoop up snow in their mittens; it was dry and flaky—not at all good for snowballs.

Father pulled Fanny up to the edge of the woods and told the girls that was as far as they could go in the sleigh. They would have to walk into the woods to find a tree. Mother stayed with the horse and sleigh and the three girls set off with their father. It was a mixed woodlot of deciduous and evergreen trees and was dark and crowded in some places. Marlene could hear squirrels chattering and see tracks in the snow. In other spots the woods were open and the trees spaced well apart. It was here that the best evergreens grew and the four began their search in earnest.

Any tree would have pleased Marlene, but Christine and Debbie were particular and found fault with every tree she pointed out. It was Father who finally spotted one that suited all three girls. It was in a small, perfect clearing with just the right amount of sunshine and space. They all stood around the tree looking at it in silent admiration. It was the right height for the parlour and the branches were spaced wide enough apart for tinsel. The homemade decorations made of bits of ribbon and lace, fruit, nuts, and berries would make the tree sparkle and shine. When Father asked if this was indeed the tree, all three sisters agreed.

He raised his axe to cut away the bottom branches to reach the stump, and a rabbit scurried out from underneath. A blue jay angrily stuck its head out from amongst the branches before taking flight. For a moment, Marlene felt her happiness drain away—

they were stealing a habitat and making the animals home-less—but Christine and Debbie assured her they would quickly find another tree to snuggle up in. With a few quick blows from Father's axe, the tree lay on the ground. The three girls grabbed the bottom of the tree and began to haul it through the woods. They didn't make it very far before they decided that perhaps it was a job best suited to Father.

When they broke free of the woods a surprise greeted them. While they were getting the tree, Mother had lit a fire and made hot cocoa, which she quickly poured into tin cups and topped with snow.

Marlene sat on the back of the sleigh drinking her cocoa, tired from the trek and thinking of the fun morning. If only every day could be like this. When everyone had finished his or her drink, Father loaded the tree onto the sleigh and began the journey home. The excitement was only half over, for the tree had yet to be stood and decorated. Then came the great fun of Christmas itself.

A Bike to Grow Into

(1964)

THIS WHOLE PROJECT BEGAN WITH THIS ONE STORY, WHICH IS MY OWN. I AM GRATEFUL FOR THOSE CAREFREE DAYS OF CHILDHOOD LONG SINCE PAST.

I wanted a bike for Christmas. It would be my sixth Christmas, and the first that I could remember wanting anything in particular. It had not been an easy choice. Ever since the Christmas catalogue arrived in the mailbox, I had spent hours poring over it seated next to the wood range. While my mother worked at the kitchen counter, I contentedly flipped through the catalogue and pondered the delights contained within. My vivid imagination took the toys right off of the pages and into the kitchen of the farmhouse. I didn't spend much time looking at dolls, dishes, or makeup kits; it was the toy trucks that drew my attention. A new one would fit perfectly with the truck and tractor already parked in the small sand pile in the corner of the kitchen.

In the end, however, I discovered my heart's desire in the toy section of Holman's Department Store in Summerside during a visit with my grandmother. I spotted a seemingly endless rack of shimmering bicycles all waiting for their future owners.

As I stood looking at the many colours of the bikes, the silver fenders, and the sturdy handlebars, my mind was made up: it was time to own a bike. I was both old enough and big enough. Besides, owning my own bike would put me on an equal playing field with my two older sisters, Debbie and Christine. Never again would I have to beg them to give me a ride on the seat of one of their bikes, nor would they be able to hide from me by swiftly pedalling away. Yes, a bicycle would be the perfect gift. I immediately asked Grandma to take me to see Santa, who was seated in the lobby outside the toy department. Santa Claus, upon hearing my request, took a long time to ponder before replying that a bike was indeed a possibility and he would see what he could do.

In the weeks leading up to Christmas, I still studied the catalogue when there was time. It was fun to dream of other presents, but my mind never strayed far from a bicycle. I was so certain Santa would fill my order that I didn't ask for anything else. Waiting was difficult. Yes, there were Christmas concerts at school, and church to take part in, and fresh snow to play in, but it was hard to concentrate. Somewhere at the North Pole, Santa's elves were building my bicycle. What colour would they paint it? Would it have silver fenders? Just how would Santa get it down the chimney?

Finally it was Christmas Eve. My sisters and I listened to the radio in the kitchen to track Santa's progress. Each time his location was mentioned, fear and delight shivered down my back and through my stomach. He was on his way! After our baths, we dressed in warm flannel pyjamas and prepared Santa's snack. Mother cautioned us to make it a small one, as the man had thousands of snacks to eat while he travelled the world. For the reindeer, we chose some slim carrots and some of the best hay from the barn. I was sure it would be the best stop of the evening for Santa's team.

Tucked up in bed, my sisters and I found that sleep refused to come. We were wide awake as if it were midday, but scared to move under our bedclothes. Every creak in the house must be Santa coming and if he caught us awake, he wouldn't leave any gifts under the tree. Dad had explained that Santa tested to see if a child was really sleeping by pulling on one of his or her big toes. The moon was high and the sky so clear that I was sure I would see Santa fly onto our rooftop and all would be lost. I buried my head under the blankets and listened to my heart pound in the stillness of the night.

The next thing I knew, my sisters were shaking me awake in the darkness of early morning to go see if Santa had come. Quietly, we tiptoed past our parents' room and down the stairs to the living room. We paused at the closed door and eyed each other. Who would be brave enough to open the door? We knew the room with the Christmas tree would be toasty warm from the big floor furnace, but was there a possibility that Santa could still be in there? Finally my oldest sister reached out and turned the knob.

At that moment it wouldn't have mattered if Santa had been in the room, for my eyes were on only one thing. Our parents had left the tree lights on and they cast a soft, multi-coloured glow. The lights shimmered on a bike standing next to the chair that held my bulging stocking. I stood frozen in place, just staring, until my sisters' squeals of delight stirred me. I moved toward the bike, afraid that it might disappear if I took my eyes off of it. When I reached out my hand and felt the cool metal in my palm, I realized it was real and I was thrilled with its beauty. It was turquoise and both the front and back fenders were brand-new, gleaming chrome. The handgrips and seat were pure white and the back fender had a red reflector. There was only one thing wrong with the bike: it was too big. It stood two feet high and it had no training wheels, but as I stood next to it I was sure Santa must have known what he was doing.

And Santa did know what he was doing according to Dad. A bike was a big gift—one that could last me a lifetime. Dad explained that Santa was not a frivolous man and believed in being practical. He knew I was growing quickly and that a small bike with training wheels wouldn't last me long. I would grow into this bike and never grow out of it. Santa Claus would have the pleasure of knowing that I would enjoy his gift for years to come. Dad explained there were a few ways for me to use the bike now, despite my small size. I could stand up while I drove, or ask my sisters for help. Dad was firm: if there was a will, there was a way.

When I had asked Santa for the bike, I had not thought about the difficulty of using it in winter. My sisters had given more thought to the season and their new sleds were perfect for zooming down the snow-covered roofs of the small outbuildings. My bike remained by the tree. Eventually, my sisters came up with an idea: who was to say a bike couldn't be ridden indoors?

Surely our mother. But it was worth a try.

My sisters carried out their plan with precision. They waited for Mother to be busy and then hoisted me up onto the seat of the bike. Christine stood on the pedals to drive. After a quick clearance from Debbie, we were off—through the living room, dining room, kitchen, and out into the porch. A quick turn took us back through the rooms to our starting spot by the Christmas tree. And there stood Mother, hands on hips, with a look of disbelief upon her face. After a moment, she began to laugh and we quickly joined her. Mother made a deal: we could ride the bike in the house as long as we didn't break anything and didn't touch the walls. I never ventured to drive the bike alone inside. I was content to sit on the seat and allow Debbie or Christine to manoeuvre along the selected path.

Winter gave way to spring and as soon as the mud dried in the farmyard, the bike was moved outdoors. It was time for me to learn to drive. Debbie and Christine took turns holding the bike as I tried to maintain my balance. Since the bike was too big for me, I could not be seated: I had to stand on the pedals, making it an even greater challenge to stay upright and get underway. When I was ready to start, a sister would run beside the bike holding it upright as I tried to get the hang of steering and pedalling at the same time.

When they thought I could balance, they let go. I would travel a few yards before crashing to the ground with the bike on top of me. Again and again we carried out this procedure and I was able to go a bit farther each time. My legs were covered in bruises but I was determined to drive that bike. With practice and patience, I could eventually drive about the yard with assistance, and then without. Finally, one day, I was able to stand on the doorstep and get onto the bike myself. Then I learned to stop by putting out my foot and touching the ground instead of simply falling over. Though I wobbled, I was driving solo.

Finally I felt confident enough to drive the bike to school. I wanted to show my classmates that I had mastered the big bike. I let Christine drive it part way with me as a passenger on the seat—but as soon as the school was within sight, I took the wheel. I swelled with pride as I pedalled down the road. The children were gathered outside and spotted me coming. They watched as I turned into the schoolyard at top speed. The grin on my face quickly disappeared when I realized I had a problem.

The school sat in a hollow with a steep driveway and the bike was gaining speed. Having no experience with using the brakes I panicked. I didn't hear my sister yelling for me to pump the brakes. I could only see my schoolmates running for cover and the schoolhouse rushing towards me. I hit it square on before toppling to the ground, the bike on top of me. As I lay there looking at the blue sky with the handlebars digging into my stomach, I sensed the others gathering around to look down at me. Seeing that I was okay they began to laugh, and I laughed the hardest of all. I had learned a lesson about showing off. I made a low-key exit from the schoolyard at the end of the day. The next day I drove the bike as far as the school entrance and then walked it down the driveway to the bike rack.

As I grew, I was able to sit comfortably on the seat and pedal wherever I wished to go. Santa was right—I had grown into the bike. It was the only one I ever owned and I drove it for years. I rode to the shore with my sisters, to the store with my friends, to the fort in the woods, to my grandparents' house, and I even taught my little sister Shelley and my cousin Sylvia how to drive using my bike. When they complained that it was too big, I told the Santa story. I explained how he was a practical man who knew they could do it if they had the will.

The years went by. The paint gradually faded, the chrome rusted, and somehow the frame got twisted, and my faithful bike was put away. One weekend when I came home from college, the bicycle was missing from its corner in the garden shed and sadness spread through me. I liked to think Santa had reclaimed it, would restore its beauty and magic, and perhaps place it by a tree for another child, one who would grow into but never grow out of Santa's bike.

Acknowledgements

To those who shared their stories and entrusted me to retell them for future generations, thank you:

Glen MacArthur Campbell
Gordon Campbell (d. 1997)
Edward Clark
Vera Yeo Forbes (d. 2015)
Olga Simpson Gamble
Claudia Cameron Kember
June Hutchinson MacLean
Glenford MacLean
Laura Millar Phillips
Edna Cameron Sheen
Melvin Stetson (d. 2015)
Jean MacArthur Yeo

I also wish to thank: my daughters, Christy and Paige, for their unlimited support; my siblings, for their continuing interest in my endeavours; and my trusted friend Alice Harnois, for her encouragement and honest feedback.

MORE FROM

Nimbus

ISBN: 978-1-77108-322-5

ISBN: 978-1-55109-943-9

ISBN: 978-1-77108-170-2

ISBN: 978-1-55109-933-0